BEATIFULLY BROKEN

THE SPIRITUAL WOMAN'S GUIDE TO
THRIVING (NOT SIMPLY SURVIVING) AFTER A
DIVORCE OR BREAKUP

MELISSA OATMAN

ISBN 978-1-989579-06-0

Ebook ISBN 978-1-989579-08-4

MotherButterfly Books

laugh.learn.love

www.motherbutterfly.com

BEAUTIFULLY BROKEN

"She is a beautiful piece of pottery, put back together by her own hands. A critical world judges her cracks while missing the beauty of how she was made whole again."

— A SPECIAL THANKS TO JAY FOR SEEING PAST THE BROKEN PIECES AND RECOGNIZING MY BEAUTY.

I would like to dedicate this book to my children, Chris and Ally. They make me want to be a better person every day. It is because of you that I chose to fix my broken pieces. I love you both with all of my heart.

A special thanks to my village; my mom, my dad, my brother and sister, my cousin Sandy and my friend Lori, who helped me raise my children and maintain my sanity in times of extreme difficulty.

Thank you to my oldest and dearest friend, Rusty, for editing my book and encouraging me to keep writing.

Without all of you I would not be who I am today.

HOW THE HELL DID YOU GET HERE?

*F*irst and foremost, I need to apologize to all of the Karens out there.

You see, I used the name Karen in my book as an example of the obnoxious, loud, horrible "friend" who always knows absolutely everything. I realize that many Karens are actually quite lovely people. So, if the Karen in your life is sweet and wonderful, then simply substitute the name Karen with the name of a horrible person in your life. I'm sure you can think of someone.

Also, I talk about the spiritual tools that you can use to help you recover from divorce, but if you are not a spiritual person, fear not; this book can still help you. You can simply choose to skip over those sections. It's none of my business if you go to hell.

I'm totally kidding. I truly believe that everyone has to do what feels right for them. My ultimate advice is to take what resonates with you and leave what doesn't.

Now, you are probably wondering to yourself, *Just what kind of book did I buy?*

Is this lady even going to help me?

Well, relax. I am totally going to help you. I just have an unconventional way of doing things. I think humor is a great way to heal. I also like to think outside the box.

Traditional wisdom is great, but have you seen any of those old psychologists giving advice lately? No, you haven't. There is a reason for that. They are all dead, and personally I would rather get advice from someone who is still in the land of the living. There is that biting humor again.

In all seriousness, though, this book is a mixture of the telling of my own story along with practical and spiritual advice about how to recover after a breakup. At the end of each chapter you will find many free tools that you can use to help you get your life back on track, and, luckily for you, I have a lot of experience when it comes to life after divorce. If you wish to follow along with the exercises at the end of each chapter, then you will need a journal, or if you are cheap, regular paper will work, and something to write with ... preferably ink and not your ex's blood.

So, sit back, relax, and enjoy this ride that we are taking together. At the end of our journey, you are going to feel so much better. Did I mention how lucky you are to have found me?

Maybe you saw the title of the first chapter and thought, *Yeah, how exactly did I end up here? How did I end up being a single mom trying to find her way back from the abyss?*

You might be feeling very confused, sad, and maybe even downright pissed off, and who could blame you? You are going through a very traumatic experience, and there is no question about that. But one thing I know for certain is that you are going to make it through this. You are going to come out on the other side of this even better than you were when you started. Your life can be absolutely amazing if you just believe it can. I am living proof that you will make it out of this mess, and your life will be even better than it was beforehand because I did it, and I know you will too.

Just how did we end up becoming this divorced and disillusioned ball of self-pity?

Why did this happen to us?

The circumstances of your divorce may differ from mine, but that really doesn't matter. We are all experiencing the same pain and anguish. The fact is that most of us are set up for disillusions about love from a young age. Most of us learned unrealistic expectations about love when we were kids.

When you were a little girl, you probably had visions of your future life and how perfect it would be. You would meet your Prince Charming. I bet you even dreamed of how he would sweep you off of your feet. You envisioned your dream wedding and dream house. Your whole life was going to be amazing. You would have the perfect family who would pose for one of those portraits where everyone is in matching outfits. Am I right?

If I didn't describe this exactly the way you imagined it, I was probably close. We all had some sort of ivory-tower fantasy growing up, and we can undoubtedly thank those awesome Disney movies or Barbie and Ken for that. Society has a way of making us feel pressured to get married as soon as we can. We just have to find that one true love.

The problem with this is that we don't really know what we want when we are young. I know I thought I knew everything at 20 years old. I learned very quickly how wrong I was. Also, there isn't just one right person for us. We have many soul mates throughout our lives, and that is perfectly OK. Who wouldn't want more people to love?

So, your perfect life wasn't perfect. This probably wasn't how you imagined it would turn out at all. I'm sure you never imagined starting your life over with young children in tow. No one ever dreams of being a single parent when they get older.

Have you ever heard of children playing divorce?

"This time I want to play the single mom!"

No, of course not.

No one thinks, *Ya know, I think I would like to do the single most challenging thing in the entire world all by myself.* And, naturally, there's a reason you didn't dream of that ... it's extremely difficult. I mean who would be crazy enough to want to do that? Seriously, who? I know I didn't.

No one ever imagines that a thing like this could happen to them. It's not something that we plan for. I was a child of divorce, and I always told myself that I would never get divorced. I would never put my own children through what I went through because I knew how hard it was for me.

The sobering reality is that sometimes we can't

prevent bad things from happening to us. We can't control every single thing that happens in life.

We can do our very best and try our hardest, and things can still not work out the way we planned. You can't control what your partner does. You can only control yourself.

I think the fact that we can't control everything in life is very frustrating for some people. How do we protect ourselves from being hurt if we can't control what happens to us?

If we could walk around wrapped in bubble wrap it would be great. The problem is you would look totally ridiculous, and you would never be able to get anything done. Plus, you would miss out on all of the good things in life, like getting hugs or back scratches.

My point is that you can't control every situation in life, and you can't shelter yourself all of the time. Besides, even if you could keep out all of the bad stuff, you would be keeping out the good stuff too. I mean, seriously, who doesn't love back scratches?

For those of us with kids, here is another thing to consider. Even though your relationship didn't work out, I'm sure you had some great memories, and now you have some amazing children too. If you didn't take the risk and enter into that partnership then you wouldn't have those beautiful faces to cherish.

You may be hurting right now, but it's going to get better.

You are going to heal from the pain of the emotional wounds because you are a tough, strong, beautiful badass.

So, you didn't choose this situation you are in, or maybe you did, but I'm sure you didn't wish to choose this. You are in it, in any case.

You can't spend the rest of your life feeling sorry for yourself. Well, actually you can, but what kind of life would that be? No one would want to be around you because you'd be a total bummer.

Your friends would start saying things like, "Don't invite Becky. She's a hot mess, and she depresses everyone." You don't want that, do you?

Take heart. There is some good news in all of this. You **can** survive. You **are** going to make it. You **are** a badass. There is nothing you can't handle. In fact, one of my favorite books is called *You are a Badass.* In it, author Jen Sincero says, "You are the only you that will ever be. You are kind of a big deal." And do you know what? She is totally right.

You are an amazing person, and you've survived so

far, haven't you? You aren't huddled in a ball on the couch sobbing your eyes out, are you? You aren't, are you? Please tell me you aren't! If you are, please stop doing that. You're being a total bummer, and you're starting to depress me.

OK, you are not really a bummer. You will have your moments when you want to curl up on the couch and cry your eyes out. Go ahead and have your pity party, Debbie Downer. That is completely normal. You do have to get those emotions out. You just can't stay in that sad state forever. You must want to feel better and get on with your life. You bought this book, didn't you? (Thank you so, so much for that, by the way.)

You are taking the steps necessary for you to heal and grow. You are a strong person, and you will make it through this. It just takes time. Taking one baby step after another you will discover that you can put your life back together again. Reading this book is the first step in the right direction.

There's a song my mom used to listen to called *One Day at a Time*. It really is true. You can make it if you take it one day, or one step, at a time. According to Kimmy Schmidt, the lead character in a show written by Tina Fey, you can make it through 10 seconds of anything. Just take it 10 seconds at a time.

Even if you are feeling overwhelmed right now, it's

all going to be OK. As Oscar Wilde once said, "Everything is going to be fine in the end. If it's not fine, it's not the end." You shouldn't worry because you are merely in the middle of your journey. You are not at the end yet.

Life is all about the journey anyway, not just the destination. You've taken a little detour for now, but your destination still awaits you. My grandma would say that you simply chose to take the scenic route. I bet that if you could see the end of your journey, you would be ecstatic at how well everything turned out.

I saw another really awesome quote the other day. It said, "Just remember that broken crayons still color." I love that. You may feel a bit broken right now, but you will still color this world. You are still valuable.

You are important, loved, and treasured. You are a child of God, the Divine, your higher power, or whatever you like to call Him/It, and you are so deeply loved. The world still needs you.

You may be a broken crayon right now, but one day you will be a whole crayon again.

When I was young, my cousin and I would melt our crayons over the heating vent in my grandma's house. My grandma was not thrilled with us, but we were able to take our broken crayons and make them whole again by melting them back together.

We performed these magical crayon operations and restored our broken crayons and made them like new again. As silly as this seems, it's quite magical really. This quote reminded me of that memory.

You too can be magically fused back together. If you work on yourself and ask your spiritual team to help, you are going to be whole once more. I promise. You still have to color this world, so get out there, you beautiful, magical crayon!

You have survived so far, and you will continue to survive. Not only will you survive, but you are going to thrive as well. Of course you are!

You were not meant to live a sad and depressing life. You are meant to flourish.

We are all here to live abundant lives full of love and magic, and you are so strong. Think of all of the things you have already made it through in the past.

You survived many horrendous things in your life like puberty, braces, your mom showing up to your school in her bathrobe (maybe that was just me) or that time you decided to put Sun In in your hair because your cousin wanted to lay out and get a tan and have blonde hair, which fried your hair and led to your two-toned hair color in the yearbook photo... I looked so hot. Maybe that was just me too. My point is that you can handle this.

You've got this! So, show some courage and stop whining. I meant that in the nicest way possible. You are going to be so awesome, and you don't even need two-toned hair or a tan for that.

Life will go on, and you will love again. I promise you will. Things will seem more normal as time goes on.

I know that may sound hard for you to believe right now, and I understand that. However, as the old saying goes, "It's hard to see the forest for the trees." I really never understood that expression when I was younger, but now I realize the true meaning.

It's hard to see past the pain when your divorce is so fresh, but there is a whole forest out there waiting for you. It might be hard for you to imagine another love and life out there for you, but it's a fact.

The amazing thing about love is that it is never far away. It might feel as though it has faded for you momentarily, yet it is simply taking on a different form. It is changing for you right now.

You may still love your ex (or you may hate them ... that's your choice ... I judge no one), but that love has to shift. It can't be the same kind of love that it once was. That hurts a lot to hear, and I sympathize with you.

The important thing for you to remember is that

even though you may not be feeling loved right now, love is always there. You will find it again. You have to believe that you are worth it, and you will be amazed at how love shows up for you. The thing we need to remember is that the most important love starts within us.

So, there is something you need to do before you even start to think about finding love again. You have to take care of something even more important first. That thing is you.

You are the most important thing right now. First and foremost, you have to take care of yourself. If you ever want someone else to love you, **you** have to love you.

You have to love yourself so much that people may start giving you weird looks. Well, forget those people. They are jerks anyway.

In this book, I will discuss how to love yourself and build your self-esteem. I also talk about getting back out in the dating game again. Besides loving yourself and having high self-esteem, another key to seeking love again, and really everything as a single woman, and perhaps also mom, is finding balance in your life. Hell, life in general is about finding balance. Balance is critical.

It's easy to allow life to wash over you like a tidal

wave and leave you looking like a drowned rat. You can either choose to ride the wave, which can be totally fun, or you can let it sweep over you and knock you flat on your face, which is totally not fun.

Plus, you will look like a drowned rat and have sand in your face, and how are you ever going to attract another partner if you look like that? It's not the most attractive look out there, sister.

But seriously, do you want to know something outrageously cool? You can have it all if you want it, and you must want it, or why would you have spent money on this book? You could have bought several cartons of ice cream instead for when you're balled up on the couch in a fetal position crying your eyes out.

I was just kidding. Don't do that.

Remember, your friends will think you are a bummer.

Please don't return this book to go get ice cream. Forget I mentioned ice cream.

Where were we? Oh yeah... I have been where you are. I have stood where you stand. I have been in the trenches during the battle of divorce. I too have felt overwhelmed by life. I have had my share of face-in-the-sand moments. I have had to pick myself up, spit out the mouthful of sand, and walk my drowned-rat-looking self back to the shore-line.

There have been many times in my life when I wondered to myself, "How did my life turn out like this? This is not at all how I imagined it would be. No one is ever going to love me again." No one plans to be a single parent. Well, maybe some people do, but those people are weird, so just forget about them. Becoming a single parent just happens ... life just happens.

You are not alone in your situation. There are many others just like you. I will show you how to pick up the pieces and find peace and balance again. I will help you to avoid all of the mistakes that I have made, and there have been many.

Hopefully, through humor and some fantastic advice, if I do say so myself, I can help you realize that it's all going to be OK. You've got this. You are a rockstar.

Your life will go on, and it's going to be amazing. It's going to be so amazing that you will wonder why you ever cared about what's-his-face in the first place. You're going to look back at this time in your life as something minor that happened to you. It was just a little bump in the road of life.

It's time to get excited. Just wait until you see your

incredible new life. It's going to be so freaking awesome. Everyone is going to be so jealous of you, especially that obnoxious know-it-all friend of yours, Karen. Well, she can suck it because your life is going to get crazy good.

2

HOW THE HELL I GOT HERE

*Y*ou may be asking yourself, "Why did I buy this book? Who is this person, and why do I trust her?" The answer is simple. I am you … all of you.

Our stories may vary, but we all share common threads. We've all had some awkward teenage experiences, some of us had older siblings who tortured us, some of us have annoying friends named Karen, but a few things we all share is that we've all gone through the awful experience of separation, and some of us are single moms as well.

Not only am I a single mom, I also grew up with a single mom. My parents divorced when I was three, so I understand how divorce feels from a child's perspective too. I have been where you stand.

I have made a lot of mistakes, and I have had many victories. My hope is that I can help you avoid the mistakes and guide you towards more victories.

My life as a single mom began for me when my children were quite small. I was 24 years old when their dad and I brought the twins home from the hospital. I remember feeling terrified, and I wondered why they would let me take them home since I obviously did not know what I was doing.

I just knew that I would surely do more harm than good for these babies because I was totally clueless. But they sent us off anyway with a look of "God help them," and we were on our way. I was sure the police knew I didn't know what I was doing. I imagined them following us home from the hospital to make sure we weren't screwing up. But no one was trailing us, and somehow I managed to keep them alive.

A year later, I was 25, a mom of twins that, despite my lack of parenting knowledge, I miraculously hadn't unintentionally harmed, and I knew I had definitely married the wrong person. Everyone says that, and it seems cliché, but I really knew I had married the wrong person.

Some people say that having a husband is like having another child, but I think mine was out to set some sort of record. I think he was going through a midlife crisis, and he was only in his 20s. It was hard enough trying to manage two kids (who were now toddlers and often crawling off in different directions) ... a grown third kid? No thanks. I didn't need the added stress in my life.

I was definitely feeling overwhelmed. On top of the fact that I had to deal with immaturity, I was also dealing with emotional and physical abuse. My ex-husband liked to play mind games and tried to control what I did. He was very good at manipulation and shifting the blame so that everything that went wrong was my fault.

It was never his fault. Plus, he was able to cry on demand, which for a long time made me feel very guilty. One day, I finally realized that he could cry at the drop of a hat, so I was pretty sure I was being manipulated. I am a very empathic person, and I don't like seeing people upset. Guess who used that against me?

I also experienced times when I felt as if I were a prisoner in my own home. If we got into an argument, he would take my car keys and unplug every phone in the house (one time even breaking my cell phone), so I couldn't call for help.

One particularly frightening experience happened for me when I was about seven months pregnant with my twins. We had an appointment to go to a non-stress test to measure the twins' heartbeats. I invited my mom to come along knowing she was excited to hear her grandchildren's heartbeats. Plus, I wanted her to be there. This set my ex off. He was livid that I had asked her to go.

He told me that it should just be our moment and to call her and tell her that she couldn't go. I refused to do that because I didn't want to hurt my mom's feelings. When I refused, we got into a very heated argument in the car. He refused to get out of my car. He asked me to come inside the house to talk. I obliged because I wanted him to get out of the car. We went inside the house, and the arguing continued. When I said I was leaving and going to the appointment by myself, he held me down on the bed in a chokehold.

I eventually broke free and drove myself to the hospital. My blood pressure was sky high, and I was having contractions. I had to be hospitalized for observations.

There were other situations similar to this, but this was definitely one that sticks out in my mind. It scared me a lot. The bad part was that I was now tied to this person I feared because we had children together. I knew that I had to eventually leave because I didn't want my daughter to think it was OK for someone to treat her that way, and I didn't want my son to think it was OK for him to treat women that way.

As parents, we are modeling love for our children. So, you should never feel guilty for leaving, even if it causes your children pain. In the long run, if you had stayed, you would have been teaching them to settle for less than they deserve.

That was my experience. The reason for your separation may differ. It's a painful experience nonetheless. It wasn't an easy choice for me to leave, as I am sure it wasn't easy for you either.

It was a very difficult time for me. I still cared very much about my ex, but I cared more about my own health and well-being.

I knew I could be a much better mom to my kids if I didn't have to worry about my partner draining me of my emotions, my finances, really anything he could take. I wouldn't have had anything left to give my children, much less myself.

Living your life emotionally drained is not living at all. I could barely function when I was in this relationship. I had blocked out all of my emotions because if I couldn't feel anything, then it wouldn't hurt so bad when my ex called me horrible names or told me I was stupid.

I became a human zombie. That is exactly how my family described me. They said, "It's like you weren't even there. Your body was there, but your mind and soul were somewhere else." I guess, in a way, I disassociated myself as a form of protection. The downside is that I blocked out all of the good memories too.

I was robbed of the memories of my sweet babies because I just disconnected myself from the whole situation. That was unfair to both me and my children. You deserve to be happy and whole. I deserved to be happy and whole. So, I left and set about trying to figure out how to be that.

Once I made the decision to leave, my life did not get easier. The first few months, even years, were a trial, to say the least. With issues like trying to raise my kids and keep them alive, my ex constantly trying to manipulate me so we would get back together or he could get whatever he wanted, tension over parenting styles and unpaid child support, it wasn't easy.

You may be experiencing this even as you are reading this. Take comfort in knowing that time will heal all wounds, and things will settle down. I realize that this sounds cliché, but it is true nonetheless.

It takes time for things to seem normal, but it will happen. You will eventually find a balance that you can live with, and as time goes on, your ex will become less emotional and be easier to deal with.

Now that I was separated, I had to start taking care of myself. Before things could get better for me, I had to decide how I was going to provide for myself and my kids. I had stayed home to take care of our twins, so I had not been working.

There was also a year where my ex didn't pay child support because he didn't have a job. This made providing for me and my kids much more challenging. Plus, there was the added bonus that my ex left me with an $8000 credit card balance. I had to figure out what to do with myself.

I think that this is a problem that many women face after divorce. We don't really know who we are besides a mom and a wife. We lose our identities somewhere along the way. I think it happens somewhere between having to wear a full figure nursing bra and pulling LEGOS out of your purse. And, somehow, I always have snacks on me too.

I needed to figure out who I was besides a mom blob. If only I could have been a beautiful, rich Hollywood starlet, life would have been so different for me. But since I couldn't be Jennifer Aniston, I had to set about finding out who I was again.

Luckily, I had a huge village around me to help. I could not have done it without my family and friends. If you don't have a village to rely on, I suggest you branch out and create your own. They are crucial to your survival. They can help you shoulder some of the burden. They can be a kind ear to listen to your worries. At the very least, they can bring you ice cream for when you are curled up on the couch in the fetal position balling your eyes out.

I thought we talked about this. I said not to do that anymore!

Deciding what to do with my life was not easy. Honestly, I had to do a little soul searching to figure out what it was I wanted to do when I grew up. I seriously felt like I was starting fresh out of high school. This was a new beginning for me. I had a college degree in German and business, but I hadn't enjoyed the business world. I mean I seriously still have nightmares about working in business, but that's a whole separate book.

I had to do something, but what could I do that would make me happy? As the saying goes, "Choose a job you love, and you will never have to work a day in your life." I really believe that there is some merit in this saying. I mean, of course, you will still have to work. It just won't suck as much if you like your job.

I remembered a job I had loved. I substitute taught when I was pregnant with my twins because I couldn't work full time, and I had really enjoyed that. I loved being around the students and soaking up their energy, even when the little kids picked their noses and wiped it on me, or when they tattled because someone cut in line, or when they wouldn't sit still in their seats because they hadn't taken their ADHD meds. Ah, the joys of teaching that you never hear about. I said I loved this job, right?

Even after experiencing snotty noses, tattle tales, and wild children, I made the decision to go back to school and get my teaching certificate. I would combine my love of German with my love of teaching and become a German teacher.

This would be easy, right? I mean what could go wrong? How hard could it be to substitute teach during the day and go back to school at night while raising two-year-old twins? Surely it couldn't be that difficult ... right?

"How stressful was it?" you ask. I had to schedule in time just to breathe some days. This was my idea, right?! I was going to be glad I did this to myself one day, right?

I still don't know how I survived this time in my life. To this day, I look back and think I must have been crazy. The bad part about it was that it was all my idea. I volunteered for this. Once again, though, my village stepped up. Without it, I probably would have forgotten to make lunches, left kids at school, forgotten my kids' names, or much worse. I don't even want to think about how much worse it could have gotten. I somehow made it through with my certificate in hand and only one forgotten lunch for what's-her-face.

Finally, I set off to find a job and try to create a somewhat normal schedule. Well, as normal as it could be raising twins. Just for your own reference, there is nothing normal about raising twins ... nothing. It's kind of like trying to staple Jell-O to the wall. Yes, it's as easy as it sounds.

After landing my first job as a German teacher, I slowly (I mean very slowly) began to settle into a routine. I was right about one thing, though; having a job you love is everything. I worked at my job as a finance manager for one year and it felt like a lifetime. I have been teaching for well over 10 years and it feels like I blinked and the time flew by.

WHAT IS YOUR PASSION?

Your passion is where you need to start in order to find the job you love, but be realistic. You can't be a police officer cowboy astronaut as my son used to aspire to be. I know we are supposed to support our children's dreams, but seriously? You gotta give me something to work with, kid.

You may already have a job you love, and that is

fantastic. If you don't love the job you have, why not try to find one you do? Maybe this divorce was a catalyst for you to find your passion.

Some of us get married young, and we don't even really know who we are yet. We are expected to pick a career at age 18, which is completely ridiculous. I was ridiculous at 18. I can't believe they trusted me to find a career path back then. I thought spray butter was the absolute best. What was wrong with me?

So many of us end up being stuck in jobs that we don't like, and that can be totally frustrating. Why not use this opportunity to start your life over? It may not be easy, but I believe that a lot of the great things in my life grew out of struggles that I over-came. It's just a thought.

Maybe take a moment to examine your current career. If you lost your job tomorrow (don't think about the financial aspect), would you feel sad, happy, overjoyed? Maybe that is telling you some-thing. I hope for your sake that you love your job and you are happy to be there. If not, maybe this is an area you could examine and possibly create a new beginning. New beginnings can be really excit-ing. It's a chance to totally reinvent yourself.

One thing I would like to point out here before we move any further is that everyone has his or her own timetable for getting through the pain of divorce.

Moving past grief is a process. We all deal with grieving in different ways.

Some people get divorced and move right along as if nothing happened. I don't personally believe this is healthy, but that is just my opinion. You do you, Karen.

I believe that if you don't heal your inner wounds, you will end up bleeding on people who didn't cut you. In other words, you are going to continue to project your pain onto your future partners. Some people take a longer time to get over their past hurts, and that is OK too. You have to decide what is best for you. There is no time limit for grief. There is nothing that says that you have to be over your hurt by a specific time.

I believe that you have to process and deal with the emotional trauma of divorce. There was probably a lesson you needed to learn there, and until you do, you are bound to repeat that lesson.

Why not take the time to regroup, figure out what went wrong, heal, and start afresh? Only you know what is best for you. You have to do what feels right for you. If it seems to take you a little longer to process what happened to you, then that is perfectly OK.

Just make sure that you aren't choosing to stay in a

place of grief and negativity. That will not help you at all. In fact, that will make you physically sick, and then, if you're a mother, you won't be able to be the best parent you can be to your children. They are counting on you because they have the best mom in the world ... am I right?

For your own sake, if it seems as though you aren't able to move past this grief, seek some professional help. There is no shame in that at all. I personally took longer than I should have to get over my grief. I chose to ignore it as if it wasn't there. I stayed so busy with life that I tried not to think about it. This is not an effective solution.

That pain does not go away. It just gets pushed down below the surface, and when you go out for drinks with friends, that stuff will come exploding out after one too many margaritas. You're going to ugly cry and probably in public. Karen will most likely post pictures of that scene on social media. She is seriously the worst.

I remember going to a club one time and they had a drag show. A bachelorette party was there, and one of the girls in it was just recently separated. Well, the performer made some comment to her, and she lost it. She ugly cried all night. I felt really bad for her, but that performer kept antagonizing her. We all wanted to say, "Look, leave her alone. She obviously isn't enjoying this." It was fairly awkward. I'm pretty sure that place went out of business too. I can't imagine why! My point is that you have to get those emotions out one way or another. I don't know about you, but I would rather not do it at a drag show.

Seriously though, you must deal with the emotions you are feeling. That is one of the reasons why I chose to write this book. I want to help others move through this more easily and with more grace than I did. Believe me, there is nothing graceful about ugly crying. So, it's important that you deal with your emotions in a way that makes you comfortable and preferably not in public, or you will end up like that girl in the example above, and I swear that girl wasn't even me, although I have ugly cried in public a time or six.

I'd like to take a moment to apologize to any friends or family I may have made uncomfortable or embarrassed by ugly crying in public. I was having a rough day. I don't want you to have to ever experience that. I wrote this book because I wanted others to feel like someone was in their corner cheering them on.

In the following chapters, I am going to give you some tools you can use to move past the emotions. These tools are totally free and they work. It is a slow and steady process, but if you do the work, you will experience a huge positive shift in your life.

So, if you really want to know who I am, I am a single mom who survived a bitter and ugly divorce. I am a Reiki Master, Life Coach, Podcaster, and Teacher. I am on a constant spiritual journey to be the best version of me that I can be.

Some people say not to let negative events change you. Well, let me tell you that my divorce did change me, but I let it change me for the better. I set out to see how I could be a better person than I was before, and I grew spiritually and emotionally.

The most important thing you need to know about me is that my life has changed in enormous ways, and I am a much better person for it. Your life can change for the better too. You can turn your tragedy into a triumph.

You too can grow and experience momentous positive shifts in your life. All you have to do is believe that you are worth it and that you can. Now, get ready for the ride of your life.

3

PARENTING

THE HARDEST TEST YOU WILL EVER FAIL

This chapter is for single moms. You can still read it even if you're not a parent. It contains helpful advice on boundaries. If nothing else, it can help you empathize with your sisters who are parenting alone.

*P*arenting is one of the most complicated, frustrating, and rewarding jobs that we will ever have. And we will all fail from time to time at parenting. That's right! I said it! You will fail at times.

You know I'm right. You always see that one post from a parent on Facebook that reads something like this: "Epic parent fail..." and you can fill in the blank with everything from "forgot to pack my son a lunch" to "I accidentally killed our goldfish." We all experience this.

I said, "We all experience this." Quit looking at me like that in judgment. I know I'm not the only one who's ever killed a beloved family pet.

I find it very interesting in our society how little we truly prepare people to become parents. It is like showing up to take a final exam for a class you never had. It's one of the most difficult and significant things you can do in life, yet you don't need any credentials to do it. You have to have a driver's license, a teaching license, and a medical license, you even have to have a fishing license, but no certification is required to be a parent.

Any idiot who can figure out how to make a baby can be one. And, no, I am not calling you an idiot ... you get the point.

Once you become a parent, you are sent out clueless trying to figure out how to keep your baby alive and make sure it doesn't grow up to be a psychopath. I mean how do people do this? Why do we do this? This wasn't my idea. I wanted a goldfish... Oh wait ... never mind.

Being a parent is one of the most important jobs there is, yet somehow we seem to forget that we need support from our village to do this job. Unfortunately, children do not come with an instruction manual. Wouldn't it be nice if they did?

A little help would've been great. I would have liked a heads-up on how to deal with projectile vomit or simultaneous leakage from every orifice, or how to put a coat on a toddler when they decide to go limp and refuse to cooperate.

They give you a 100-page manual on all of the features of your new car, yet they send you home from the hospital with your kid and give you a smile and a look that says, "God help them."

You would never walk into a high-demand job and say, "I don't need training, and I don't need any help." Any good leader knows that you need a team who supports you, and you need to know what the hell you are doing. Moms are not different.

Think of this as a corporation that you are the head of. You need a strong team to help you manage. I mean you are in charge of little people who somehow managed to be born smarter than you. How did they figure this stuff out? Who teaches them that go limp routine anyway? It's genius. Can you just picture adults doing that? I'm going to try that next time my boss says I have to go to a faculty meeting and I don't wanna go. On second thought, I enjoy being employed. I'd better not try that.

My point is that moms need to stick together. We have a tough job, and society does not make it easier for us. We get judged and blamed for everything, from our kids eating Tide pods to our kids doing some stupid YouTube challenge. They never told me that this could happen in my childbirth class. I mean, seriously, what kid does that? I blame the mom. She obviously doesn't know what she is doing.

The grim reality in society about being a single mom is that we tend to take the blame or are made to feel guilty about anything that doesn't measure up with our kids. If our child isn't perfect, some people in society will say, "It had to be the mom's fault. She must have failed at her job. That child probably comes from a broken home."

Can I just take a moment to say that I hate that phrase? How stupid is that? I picture a house where one side fell over. Could we possibly come up with a more offensive and idiotic phrase? My home is perfectly unbroken, thank you. How dare you make fun of my house?

Being a parent is stressful no matter what your home situation is like. I know plenty of couples who are both equally bad parents. Why do you have to be single to suck at parenting?

It's like an unwritten law that your divorce had something to do with your child's problems. Maybe my child would have been a psychopath anyway,

Karen. Maybe I would have sucked at this even if I did have a husband. Did you ever think about that?

Once you are a mom, nothing else seems to matter. If you made the newspaper for anything, it would simply read, "Mom of Two Does... (fill in the blank)." It doesn't matter if it's good or bad, you will be forever known as "Mom of Two or Three or Four or Five ... haven't you ever heard of birth control?" I'm just kidding. Go ahead and have five kids. God help you.

I'm certain that they have come up with studies that show that children of single parents commit more crimes than any other group. You name it, and they will blame us for it. Think about it; you probably judge other moms too. When you read news stories, I'm sure you have thought to yourself, *What was that mom thinking?*

I'll bet you were wondering in the paragraph above about the Tide pods. Well, stop judging them ... it's a tough job. Good people accidentally kill family pets, Karen! Stop looking at me like that.

We have to support one another. We need to be one another's biggest cheerleaders. Society may try to make us feel like failures, but we can't let it. You haven't failed. None of us have. Being a parent is one of the toughest jobs there is, even for people who are married and both there for their kids full time. Being married doesn't automatically make you a great parent. You can still screw that up, believe me!

However, being a parent and going through a divorce is more challenging than usual. You will learn to navigate those waters just fine. Even I tell myself every day that I am doing the best I can for my kids, and if I buy a new goldfish they will never know. If you do happen to fall (and we all do at times), get back up; pull that Tide pod out of your child's mouth, adjust your crown, and move on. You are a queen and deserve to be treated as such.

There are a lot of resources out there for you that can help. Support groups are a great way to meet other moms like you. Finding a support group for single moms is a great opportunity for you to hear how other moms are coping, and you can get some great ideas. There are a lot of online social media groups that are free to join. It's also a way for you to hear about the struggles that others are going through, and this will at least help you to understand that you are not alone in this grueling process that we call parenting. Other people are screwing up just as much as you are. You may even find that some people are way worse than you. Take Karen, for example. She is the absolute worst.

$\sim$

BOUNDARIES

Kids need to feel secure, and one way to do that is to set healthy boundaries for them. When I say boundaries, what I mean is setting rules. It is completely healthy and normal for kids to try to push boundaries or break rules because they are learning who they are. If you don't set boundaries for them, then how will they know when they are crossing a line with their behavior?

It can lead to confusion and insecurity in your child if you don't have set boundaries. They will act out because they don't know what makes you mad from one day to the next, and they don't know what punishment they will receive from one day to the next. There is too much inconsistency.

If you don't have rules, or if you are constantly yelling at your kids and parenting them based on emotion, your children are more likely to internalize the punishment. They may take your yelling and emotional outburst as a direct reflection of how you feel about them. This can lower their self-esteem.

In setting rules for them, you are actually making them feel safer, more secure, and loved. You are also teaching them how to set healthy boundaries for themselves. When you can take the emotion out of punishing them, you won't have to yell and get upset when they break a rule because they already know what the punishment will be for crossing that line. All you have to do is let them know that they crossed it. It becomes a much calmer and more effective way to parent.

We have to set boundaries for them, and sometimes that can be uncomfortable for both you and your children. Plus, if you grew up in a home like I did where there were no boundaries, it can be hard to figure out how to set your own.

Let me give you an example. When I was growing up, we didn't have a specific set of rules to follow. We just knew we had crossed a boundary if our mom's face turned purple and she started screaming. We only figured out where the boundary was by crossing it, and the boundary was different from day to day. If she was tired, then more things irritated her. In the same way, she used to punish us based on emotion and not logic.

This made punishment very random. It always depended upon her mood. That isn't a very stable way to parent, but many people do it this way. It is very easy to fall into this type of parenting style because you do whatever is most convenient at the time. It will most definitely lead to frustration and confusion though.

My kids' dad wasn't always supportive with rules. I

used to want to give in to them because I felt guilty about being the mean parent while their dad was the fun parent. I can't tell you how many times I heard that I was the worst parent ever. You should realize that if you hear this, it probably means you are doing your job.

You will have a lot of bumps in the road as a parent, it's natural. Never give up. No matter how much you think you can't do this—know that you can. There are a lot of really great parenting books and other resources out there to help you.

One book I really loved is called *Boundaries with Teens* by John Townsend. I discovered it when I was desperate to find a way to reach my hard-headed son. It's a great book for learning how to set boundaries and rules for your teenage children.

There is also a book called *Boundaries with Kids.* I highly recommend these books because I wasn't prepared for setting and keeping rules with my kids because I never had clear rules myself growing up. I knew I crossed a boundary at the moment I crossed it. We didn't have set rules. We just knew if my mom started yelling it would be a good time to start running.

I know this is a lot to process. Don't worry. You will be great. Just know that there are many awesome resources out there for parents. Find the groups that resonate with you. You can even search online to find parenting resources available in your area. You will be amazed at how much is out there, and much of it is free. So keep on being the rock star mom I know you are.

4

LOVING YOURSELF

LIKE THE TRUE NARCISSIST YOU ARE

I'm sure you read the title of this chapter and thought, *What? I'm not a narcissist! Those people are the worst. Karen is the narcissist. She is so arrogant. She just loves to talk about herself and all of her accomplishments. No one can stand her.* Well, Karen may be a narcissist; however, loving yourself doesn't make you one.

Many people associate having high self-esteem with being conceited or being a narcissist, and this simply is false. While it is true that some people outwardly love themselves just a little too much (I'm sure we all pictured a few specific celebrities; an orange one with bad hair comes to mind), it is also extremely crucial that you love yourself. You don't have to brag about everything that you do all day long, and you aren't being conceited. And, anyway, most people who really are true narcissists suffer from other mental issues, and that is not you. That is only Karen and the orange-tinted minion.

Before you can start putting your life back together again, it is crucial to think about your own needs. You have to know who you are before you can really be who you are.

Psychologist Abraham Maslow created a hierarchy of needs. In that hierarchy, Maslow identified the basic needs that motivate us. Those needs are physiological, which are basic essentials like food and water. We need to feel safe, we need love, and we need to have a high amount of self-esteem and a high amount of self-actualization, which is the degree to which we feel we can achieve our goals and reach our full potential as human beings.

Obviously, we know that we need love. We need to be able to give love and receive love. What we often forget, though, is that in order to do that, we have to feel that we are worthy of it. That is where that self-esteem is so critical. If you don't have high self-esteem and you don't feel worthy of love, how can you expect someone else to see you as worthy of love?

We don't often think about our need for being loved as being met by ourselves, but that's exactly where it has to start. No one else can make you feel whole and complete. You have to do that on your own. You have to know that you are awesome and feel that you can achieve anything that you wish to accomplish. If you have low or no self-esteem, you are setting yourself up to live a life of just meh.

Also, you will be more likely to attract someone who isn't worthy of you. We are all made up of energy, and our energy enters the room before we do. Our energy is actually what attracts people to us. I'm sure that you have met people you instantly didn't like but didn't know why. It was because you were picking up on their energy.

When you don't love yourself, or you feel like you don't deserve love, you give off a very low vibrational energy. It's essentially the same as walking into a room and saying, "Don't bother looking at me. I'm not that great and I'm not worth your time." Of course, we know this isn't true. However, it is the energy that you are giving off. Therefore, you are attracting people who either have this same energy or who are looking for people they can prey on. People who manipulate others usually prey on those with low self-esteem.

On the contrary, many highly successful individuals find high self-esteem and confidence very attractive. That's right; people who are secure in themselves attract more people, and, more importantly, better people.

I know you want to attract the right kind of relationship, so you may be asking yourself, *How can you get self-esteem if you don't have it?* Are you a lost cause?

No, you are absolutely not a lost cause. Many of us have low self-esteem because of issues that stem from our childhood or even on a deeper level, our past lives. We might not even realize that we have low self-esteem. You may see yourself as being flexible or accommodating and not even realize these are traits of people with low self-esteem. You may also feel high amounts of anxiety.

Do you worry a lot? Are you worried that you worry? Just kidding. Now I sound like one of the prescription drug commercials. Seriously though, anxiety is also a trait of people with low self-esteem. I should know. I definitely suffered from low self-esteem, and I still battle self-doubt from time to time. I really hope you are liking my book right now. You see what I mean?

Most people experience self-esteem or self-doubt. It's a very common problem. Fortunately, there are many things you can do to increase your self-esteem and to quiet those fears and doubts. Don't beat yourself up over your shortcomings. Remember ... you are a badass! You're awesome, and everyone loves you. Everyone has something that they would like to change about themselves. It's learning how to love every part of ourselves, even our flaws, that matters.

Loving yourself isn't being conceited. It increases our self-esteem when we love ourselves, plus you are fulfilling a most basic need, which is the need to be loved. Most people falsely believe that this need is met by others, but, in actuality, you have to meet this need within yourself first before you can truly receive love from others.

You've probably heard that "You complete me" line in the movie *Jerry Maguire*. The problem with that line is that no one should ever complete you. They can complement you, but you should be a whole or complete person on your own. If you do feel as though you have a void in your life, you have to be able to fill that void yourself.

"So, what does this mean, and how do you fill the void?" I'm so glad you asked. That was a great question. You are so smart. Please allow me to explain.

SELF-ESTEEM

We discussed that one of Maslow's needs in his hierarchy of needs is self-esteem. Loving yourself absolutely contributes to your self-esteem. If you have low self- esteem, then you probably beat yourself up on the regular with your own thoughts.

Have you ever thought to yourself, *I'm not good enough,* or *I'm not as good as so and so*? You may worry often or be anxious. Maybe you doubt your decisions or don't make any at all because you think you will make a mistake.

You may also try to be too accommodating for others without taking your own feelings into consideration. Do any of these things sound familiar? If so, then you probably suffer from low self-esteem.

This is nothing to be embarrassed or upset about. Many people have battled with low self-esteem, myself included, and there are many reasons we suffer from this. One major reason is that we carry things over either from our childhood or from past lives.

Sometimes things that happen to us when we are young leave a lasting effect on us, and we don't even realize it. If you had very strict parents who yelled at you a lot (I'm fairly certain that this was pretty much our entire generation), it is possible that this form of discipline made you feel unworthy or not good enough.

Sometimes parents also have extremely high expectations for us, and if we don't meet those expectations, we may feel as though we disappointed them. Have you ever heard your parents say, "I'm disappointed in that grade; I know you can do better"? That can also make us feel less worthy of love. Were you ever compared to a sibling? This also causes us to doubt ourselves.

In addition, if you had parents who didn't set healthy boundaries, then you probably internalized a lot of the punishments you received as well. I talked about how that affects children in the last chapter.

Having no rules probably caused you to feel insecure because there was no stability in the way your parents punished you. Parents mean well, but the more we learn about parenting styles, the more we realize that there are better ways out there. I'm not blaming anyone because I absolutely believe that all parents are trying to do the best that they know how. Some parents are just better equipped to do this than others.

Most of our parents learned their parenting styles from their parents. It's a vicious cycle. So, next time you see your grandparents, tell them how you can thank them for your low self-esteem. I'm totally kidding. Don't you dare do that to Nana and Papa. Now she's crying. Why were you so mean to Nana?

In all seriousness, our past can definitely influence

our present. If you had any traumatic events in your childhood, then it would certainly stand to reason that you may be feeling the effects of that today. You may be carrying around trauma that you do not even remember. This trauma could be from your childhood or it could stem from a past life as well.

Obviously, we do not remember our past lives, but our cell memory exists. Memories can be stored at the cellular level, so we may not remember them, but our bodies do. Even if we don't remember things that have happened to us, our body reacts as though we do. It's possible that you could be bringing memories over from past events.

If you are experiencing self-esteem problems but you really can't think of any good reason why, it's probably a cell memory. You can do a past life regression (either through your own meditation or with a professional) to see if you can figure out what triggered that low self-esteem.

Most of us can attribute low self-esteem to events that have happened in this lifetime. For me, a combination of many events led to my low self-esteem. The first event was the divorce of my parents. Again, I would like to stress that I don't blame them. Being a divorced parent, I totally understand now why it was necessary.

However, the little girl in me didn't understand why

my dad was leaving. I carried that memory with me at the cellular level. I even remember feeling like I was somehow responsible for their divorce, like I should have prevented it, even though there is no way a three-year-old could have done anything to alter this. This event truly affected me. Although I had to go on with my life, I was still holding on to that memory without realizing it.

I was also from the generation of parenting with such wisdom as, "I'll give you something to cry about. I brought you into this world and I'll take you out," and other gems like that. You know, very uplifting and positive messages. I'm sure that those expressions helped me to feel like the princess I was. Yeah ... not so much. Being a single mom, my mom never had time to sit down and come up with rules for us. We didn't know where our boundaries were and punishment was often inconsistent.

We already talked about how that leaves kids feeling insecure. I know my mom did the best job that she could. I know that her parents were fairly inconsistent at parenting too, and she did not have a particularly easy childhood either. Additionally, I was a very shy teenager, and I didn't date much in high school. I had acne and braces. I was not exactly Cover Girl material, and on top of that I had Sun In damaged hair. This definitely did not help my self-esteem.

The major factor that really caused my self-esteem to plummet through the floor was my marriage to my ex. I'm sure that my already low self-esteem helped me to attract someone who could be manipulative and at times verbally abusive. We attract the energy that we put out. So, if my energy was that of someone with low self-esteem, guess what I attracted. You guessed it.

I attracted someone with low self-esteem. If I didn't act the way that he thought I should, then I would be called horrible names or told that I was (fill in the blank with any vile thing you can think of here). That did wonders for my self-esteem. People who have low self-esteem are often the bullies of this world. It makes them feel better about themselves to bully others.

In my case, I was simultaneously told I was an angel and then called a bitch. That sent a very mixed message. I don't want to dwell on this because I have already forgiven my ex, he has apologized, and I don't blame him. We were both immature, we didn't know how to communicate, and he was going through his own stuff at the time. It doesn't really matter at this point anyway. I'm just trying to point out the reasons why I suffered from self-esteem issues.

One of the things that you can do to help heal some

of the wounds that are causing your low self-worth is to forgive others who need it. There are so many benefits to forgiveness.

Forgiveness removes the heaviness caused by emotional wounds that we are carrying around with us. So, if forgiveness is so great, why do we find it extremely difficult to forgive others? I mean for some of us it is the most difficult thing that we will ever have to do.

I believe that one reason some people have a hard time forgiving others is that they feel that if they forgive someone they are saying that the behavior that needs forgiveness is excused. This simply isn't true. By forgiving others, you aren't saying that what the person did is OK. You are simply allowing yourself to be free of the burden of carrying around the pain that it caused.

Forgiveness is more about you than the other person. Carrying around all of those negative and bitter feelings is going to cause you emotional and physical distress. I was listening to a podcast and the host, who is a psychologist, mentioned that people who forgive are less likely to develop health problems such as high blood pressure. I even read a theory that cancer and forgiveness are related. I don't know how true this is, but it was an interesting argument.

Being upset at someone causes negative emotions. Negative emotions will definitely make you sick. It makes sense that if you are able to forgive and let go, you will feel better both physically and emotionally. Not to mention that it will raise your energy vibration to let go of all of that emotional junk.

Plus, when you refuse to forgive others, you are keeping yourself connected to the people who wronged you energetically. It's hard to imagine what carrying around energy is like, so let me give you a mental image. Picture yourself dragging around the bodies of all who have hurt you. Energetically that is what you are doing.

Those people are holding you back from truly living. Do you really want to hang on to all of that negative energy? That would certainly get old and heavy fast. Some people also fear that if they forgive others, they are opening themselves up for the bad behavior to happen to them again. This is not the case.

We experienced the hurt in the first place because we had some sort of lesson to learn. Once we forgive and learn that lesson, we can move on. When we ask for help in that forgiveness, it's amazing what happens.

My dad and I were able to get together and talk about his and my mom's divorce and ask each other for forgiveness for our past behaviors. It was very healing, and I am able to have a better relationship with him now, which I love.

Another way to ensure that your self-esteem stays intact is to watch how you talk to yourself. You need to think and talk positively about yourself. Using a mantra is a great way to change your self-talk. A mantra is something that you say to yourself throughout the day to help you stay positive. It can be anything you want; however, the important thing is to make sure that it is something that will lift you up.

You will also have to learn how to change your story. We all have that broken record in our heads that says we are not good enough, smart enough, or (fill in your own insecurity here). We need to learn how to change that record and write a new story for ourselves. We'll talk more about how to do that in a little bit.

Furthermore, it is also extremely important that you do not compare yourself to others. We are all here on our own individual journeys. We all have different road maps for how and when we will achieve certain goals. Do not worry about keeping up with anyone else. That's right, Karen. We don't have to be as good as you. Be true to yourself. Remember, "You are the only you that will ever be." You are definitely a big deal.

It is super important to always be conscientious about what you do every day. One thing that will help you to keep your sanity is to realize that you are human. You would be amazed at how many people forget that. You are going to have some missteps. Do not strive for perfection. It's unrealistic, and you will drive yourself insane. Perfection is just another form of anxiety anyway. I do not know any perfect people. I only know people who think they are perfect (that's right, Karen, I called you out!), and those people are definitely not perfect. They are perfectly obnoxious. We all make mistakes, which brings up another important point. Whatever you do, do not beat yourself up for your blunders. There are no wrong choices.

∾

CELEBRATE THE JOURNEY

Our journey is like a map. If you make a wrong turn, you will still get to your destination. You just took a different course. My grandma would say that you took the scenic route. I've taken the scenic route so many times that my GPS yells at me now. "No, you idiot, I didn't say turn left. I said right." Sometimes I just like to challenge it to see if it can keep up with all of my bad choices in real time. I've heard "rerouting" so many times that I literally hear it in my head now when I know that I probably made a mistake.

One of the best trips I ever took had my friend and me in tears laughing about how bad my sense of direction is. We still laugh about it to this day. My ex-husband used to ask, "Which way should I turn?" and I would say, "Left," and then he would go the opposite way. Of course, it worked. So, you see it's no big deal. Don't sweat the small stuff. The only wrong choice you can make is not making a choice at all.

You are going to take some wrong turns in life. We all do. It doesn't make you a failure. Mistakes are how we learn, plus many awesome things were created from mistakes.

Take Milk Duds for instance. The name says it all. They were not supposed to look like they do (they were duds), but here they are, and they are delicious anyway.

I'm from St. Louis, and we are known for our toasted ravioli. This was another brilliant creation conceived in error. A regular ravioli was dropped into the fryer by accident and viola—the best fried appetizer around. Sometimes out of mistakes our best ideas are born.

One sure-fire way to keep your self-esteem up is to celebrate your victories no matter how small they are. They are important. Sometimes they can be very small.

For instance, if I walk into the kitchen with a cup in my hand to put in the sink and I walk back in the living room without the cup because I actually remembered why I walked into the kitchen in the first place, I celebrate that. I am surprised I remembered to put the cup in the sink in the first place, and I didn't get sidetracked by 50 other things, or if I get to a destination without hearing "Rerouting," I'm celebrating for sure. You may be making fun of me right now, but I seriously feel like that is a celebratory moment.

What do you do that is worth celebrating? Sometimes, all it takes is that I wasn't balled up on the couch crying my eyes out today. It's the little things in life. I know you have some awesome stuff to celebrate, so celebrate away. Get in the habit of doing that.

One of my favorite Disney parades of all time had a song that was called "Celebrate You." I loved that song, and sometimes I would just turn it up really loud and sing it at the top of my lungs. It really is true though. Now is the time to celebrate you. Find that song, turn it up, and do a parade around your living room, you beautiful badass!

Self-Care

Doing things for yourself is another way to boost your self-esteem. You should treat yourself like the goddess you are. Something you can do to be good to yourself is to be kind to your body. One of the things you can do to treat your body right is to work out.

Try to work out a few times a week if you can. Those endorphins that are released during exercise will give your mood a boost in the right direction. Plus, if you celebrate how strong and dedicated you are for working out, you will feel like a rock star. You will feel super sexy with your new hot body, and your ex will be foaming at the mouth. That poor idiot. Try to eat healthy too. Healthy food doesn't have to taste bad. Look for some new recipes online. I love spending time on Pinterest searching for new ideas.

Sometimes when we constantly put crap into our bodies, it can make us feel sluggish and depressed. Try to avoid a lot of processed foods if you can. I know that it is not always possible, but even reducing the amount that you eat will help. You can even do this in small steps. If you eat fast food every day, then maybe cut down to every other day or do it one less day a week.

Our body needs the proper fuel, and when we eat processed food, it's like putting bad gas in our cars. You will run much better on foods that are good for you.

Get the right amount of sleep when possible too. Lack of sleep can mess up our bodies in many ways.

Drink a lot of water. Ideally, we should drink eight eight-ounce glasses a day. This is one area that I have a hard time with because water has no taste ... I mean zero taste. You can infuse it with natural ingredients, though, to make it better.

I like adding strawberries and fresh basil to my water, I also slice lemons and add fresh mint. Fresh fruit of any kind will help flavor that water. Get creative here. You can come up with a lot of different flavor combinations.

Pamper your skin too. Give yourself a homemade facial or buy one of those masks at the store. If you drink lots of water and use masks on your face, you will see a marked improvement in your skin. If there are positive changes that you can make in your life, then by all means make them.

You don't have to do a lot of things at once. Just start small, and try to do things that make you feel good. Your body will thank you, and Karen may try to spread rumors that you have had some work done, but forget her. She is the worst... Am I right?

HELPING OTHERS

Many people feel better by giving back to their community or favorite charity. This is a great way to feel good about yourself. Some people give money, which is great, but giving your time is sometimes needed more and will make you feel as though you have accomplished something awesome.

Helping others makes us feel better about ourselves, and we are contributing to society in a positive way. You don't have to think of some grand idea to help either. If you have one, that is great, but it is perfectly OK to start small. Donate an hour of your time at a local food bank. Clean out your closet and give the clothes to an organization that helps others.

If you're not sure where to start, you can go to your community's website and see if there are any charitable organizations listed or any volunteer opportunities. Every little bit helps, and it will definitely give you a sense of self-worth and purpose in your life. We all need that. If you already do these things, then I applaud you. You are awesome! Way to go! You are killing it! I celebrate you!

Doing any of the things suggested above is sure to help you increase your self-esteem. It should also help you to know that I think you are really brave for trying to get on with your life. After a divorce, it could be so easy to bury your head in the sand and just go through the motions in your life.

The fact that you are trying to make your life better speaks volumes about you. You are courageous, intelligent, beautiful, and creative. I know that you may be hurting right now. It can feel as though you have the weight of the world on your shoulders, and you may feel like your heart will never feel whole again, but you will get through this. It's going to be OK.

I promise you that all is not lost. You are a wonderful person. You should think highly of yourself because I know that I think highly of you, and I know that God thinks highly of you too. Our entire spiritual team wants us to live a life of extreme prosperity. They want you to be so freaking happy. You deserve it, and it is going to happen for you.

JOURNALING MOMENT

SELF ESTEEM

I am giving you a homework assignment. That's right. I'm a teacher, and it's what I do. Besides, journaling is a very easy and positive way to help us work through difficult situations and emotions.

So, get a journal. If possible, get one that you really like. I have one that has a quote from Walt Disney on it. It says, "If you can dream it, you can do it." I love that. That is one of my mantras for my life.

I want you to write in a journal all of the things that you can think of that may have affected your self-esteem. When you are finished, read over what you wrote.

Think about your own life and what may have triggered your self-esteem issues.

Did you have people who called you names or talked down to you?

Maybe there were people who thought they were protecting you by saying things such as, "Don't get your hopes up too high. You have to be realistic." Those expressions are meant to help us stay grounded and protected, but they really cause us to doubt ourselves.

Were you constantly being compared to someone else? I know that grade comparison is a mistake I made with my kids.

Maybe you had a traumatic situation happen to you in your past and you never really dealt with the effects of it.

AFTER-JOURNALING REFLECTION
FORGIVENESS

Depending on what you wrote in your journal, there are different things that you can do to help you increase your self-esteem.

If your self-esteem problems stem from an incident in your past, like divorce (I was holding on to hurt feelings with my dad because I didn't fully understand his role in my parents' divorce), then forgiveness for the past hurt might be helpful for you.

There is an excellent website called *Radical Forgiveness*. It's a wonderful site where they explain that many of the hurts that we are holding on to can be let go simply by realizing that our souls have made pacts with other souls to come here on Earth and experience situations together in order for our souls to grow and elevate. They have free worksheets on this site to help you work through forgiveness for anyone you need to forgive.

What that means is that my soul and my dad's soul made an agreement to come here and go through the experience of this divorce so that we could both learn and grow from it. It makes sense if you think about it, and when you look at it from that perspective, it takes away the pain and the raw emotion.

The great thing about it is that the party you need to forgive doesn't even have to participate in this. They do not even need to know you did it. This forgiveness is for you anyway, not for the other person. You can do this for as many people as you need to.

We have so many resources to help us find forgiveness. For instance, you can also ask your angels and guides to help you forgive someone. Archangel Uriel is the angel associated with forgiveness. Ask Archangel Uriel to be with you as you pray for forgiveness or go through the steps of forgiveness for any person. Uriel is associated with the color amber, so you may see or sense pale yellow when praying. The angels are happy to help us, but we must ask them for it. I think it is interesting that we learn about angels in church and they are all throughout the Bible, but then they are never mentioned when we pray. That makes no sense. Praying for help from our angels and guides is one of the best ways to receive help and guidance. They love helping us, but we have to ask them for it. They can't intervene simply because they want to do so. They have to know that we want and need their help.

> *A Prayer to Archangel Uriel:*
> *Archangel Uriel, I call on you today and ask that*
>   *you help me to forgive any person who has*
>   *done me harm. I ask that you release me of*
>   *the emotional burdens that I am carrying*
>   *from this hurt. Please release me from all fear*
>   *and emotional blocks. Allow me to feel peace*
>   *and love in my heart once more.*
> *Amen*

Another tool that you have in your arsenal and that you can use is your spiritual team. You can ask your angels to help you love yourself more. Archangel Chamuel heals anxiety and shows us how to love ourselves more. Say a prayer to him to help you learn to love yourself better. He appears as a pale green light, so you may sense or see this color as you pray to him. In addition, I'm giving you another homework assignment: Quit groaning. It's good for you.

JOURNALING MOMENT

NEGATIVE AND POSITIVE

In your journal, make two columns. In the left-hand column, write down any negative thoughts that you have about yourself throughout the day. You can either write them as you think them or wait until the end of the day to write them down. Look at what you wrote. What things are you saying about yourself?

Now write a different, positive version next to the original thought in the right-hand column.

Here is an example: In the left-hand column, you write, "I am so disorganized." In the right-hand column, you write, "I am so intelligent that I have many things going on at one time."

You see what I did there? I took something that I might have seen as a negative in myself and put a positive spin on it. It's really all about learning how to change your perspective.

AFTER-JOURNALING REFLECTION

SAY GOODBYE

Once you have looked at your lists, look at what you are saying to yourself every day.

What lies do you keep repeating to yourself about you? Now look at the positive side. These are the core beliefs that you are going to begin telling yourself. After you have had time to observe your thoughts, cut out the negative column and either burn it or tear it up. You are done telling yourself those lies. Buh bye.

5

FINDING PEACE

AFTER PICKING UP THE PIECES

So, just how do you find your peace after going through the trauma of divorce? Some people may balk at my use of the word trauma to describe divorce, but anyone who has ever been through it knows that this is the perfect word. Everything is chaotic.

Your life will never again be the same as it was. It can feel as if your world has been turned upside down. The process of divorce is usually full of tense arguing, and the reality is that you now have to create new boundaries with your ex.

This person who was supposed to be your best friend and partner for life has likely now become more like an enemy. This is the sad realization that many of us have faced, yet it doesn't have to be a sad thing.

Of course, you will experience the pain and anguish of loss. That is perfectly normal. What I mean is ... what if you choose not to stay sad? What if you shifted your perspective? What if instead of seeing this as something negative, you saw this as something positive?

That may sound absurd to you right now. I totally understand that. However, if you were to change your viewpoint, you would see that there are miracles hidden in every experience, even the ones we think of as negative. That may seem like a strange statement, but it is true. Your divorce could be a miracle in disguise.

This could be an opportunity for your soul to grow. This might be a chance for you to be happy again. What if you were leaving an average marriage to find an extraordinary life, which could include an even more harmonious and freaking amazing marriage? Wouldn't that be awesome?

SHIFT THE ENERGY

One of the ways we can change our viewpoints is to shift our energy. You may be wondering what in the world I am talking about. "What does this shifting your energy business even mean?" Well, I am so glad you asked. Did I mention how smart you are?

We are all made up of energy. Every single one of us is just a big ball of energy. After traumatic events like divorce, our energy can shift down into a lower vibration. As you may have realized, having a lower energy vibration is not what you want. You wouldn't want to have a lower bank account balance, would you? No, of course not.

Remember playing Super Mario Brothers when you were a kid (I may be dating myself here)? Every time something hit you, you would lose power. You earned more points at the end of each round if you had all of your power intact. Think of your energy in the same way. The higher your vibration (or the more power you have), the better you will be.

If you were to shift your energy from lower to higher vibrations, you would be amazed at how your life would change. The other interesting thing about shifting our energy is that it causes the energy of the people around us to shift too.

Having a higher energy vibration could help make the process that you are going through easier and less painful. I'm not saying you won't experience pain because we all have to experience some pain in order to grow, but it would make your experience easier. You would probably experience less stress too, and who doesn't want that?

NEW MINDSETS

It could also be a great excuse for you to create a new and better version of yourself. Think of it like buying an awesome new outfit, except the new outfit isn't for your body, it's for your soul. You could have everything you ever wanted from now on simply because you decided to change your mindset.

Your old mindset probably included ideas like, *What if I never recover from this? My life is over now. I will never find love again. I will never be the same.*

What if I told you that not being the same again wasn't a bad thing? Seriously, this could be a good thing for you. Did you ever think about that? What if this divorce was a chance for you to discover who you are and who you want to become?

What if you were just coasting along in life? I mean you may have been happy, but were you really fulfilled? Were you really experiencing all that the world has to offer?

We were not meant to live a life of just ordinary, yet most of us walk through life doing just that. People go to their jobs that they tolerate or to their spouses who are nice, but there is no excitement there. They are simply appeased with a mundane existence. That is not what this life is all about.

We were sent here to live extraordinary lives full of love and abundance, but some of us are not experiencing that. Sure, we may be content, but we are not experiencing our true bliss. You deserve to be the happiest person you can be. I know you are not going to argue with me about that. Everyone wants to find happiness, and everyone deserves to find it. The interesting thing about this is that we actually form our own reality based on our thoughts.

God does not want us to experience a meager existence, yet most of us are content to do just that. I think that this makes God sad because He created us with such love. He sees just how special we are. Remember, you are kind of a big deal. I'm sure that He wants to see all of our dreams fulfilled. In fact, He wants to help us do that. He wants us to be so elated that we will wonder why we were ever satisfied living an average life in the first place.

It's not just God who wants to help. We have a whole spiritual team who wants to help us live out our life's purpose. So, why do we walk through life being complacent? Why don't we want abundance? Why are we OK with just average?

Rude Awakenings

One thing I have noticed when I start to get too comfortable is that life does something major to shake me up and get my attention. How rude! Imagine a huge arm coming down and slapping you as hard as it can to wake you up. That's what it feels like sometimes.

On occasion, the wake-up call that we get is when something really awful happens in our lives ... you know, like divorce. That huge slap upside the head is necessary for us, though, because when we become complacent, we aren't experiencing all of the joys that life has to offer. We walk through life with blinders on, and we don't fully realize how beautiful life truly is.

We aren't seeing our talents being used to their full potential. We need those events in our lives that we often feel are tragedies in order to re-evaluate our lives. We need to examine whether or not we are truly sharing our gifts with the world.

Imagine if someone was a gifted artist but they chose only to paint at home by themselves and never shared their gifts with others. The world would miss out on all of that beauty. There have probably been a lot of people who never discovered or shared their talents with the world. What a wasted gift that is. We are all gifted in some way or another. Even if you think you have no talents or gifts, I assure you that you are mistaken. Everyone has a gift.

Here is a question for thought. How happy were you in your life and marriage? Many people put on a brave face and say they are content, but underneath that facade they feel a certain void.

I can't tell you how many people I have talked to who tell me that they feel very alone in their marriages, but they stay in them because they are comfortable. I would venture to say that there are many people who stay in marriages that are unfulfilling for the simple reason that change is too scary. It's not that there's anything wrong with being comfortable per se. It's just that I would hate to think that someone missed out on an opportunity to experience total fulfilment because they were too fearful to take a risk. That is so sad. I mean life is awesome!

We should be overjoyed with our lives. That's not to say that we won't ever have problems, but we should feel blessed every day. When we don't stop to appreciate how awesome the world is, I think it pisses the Universe off. I think the Universe is telling us to wake up and see who we were designed to be. It wants us to stop living a mediocre life.

Think about it, most of us would never move out of

our comfort zones unless we were forced to do so. Sometimes I believe that this is why tragic events like divorce happen to us. Really, we should see that they are not happening **to** us but **for** us.

This is the Universe's way of telling you to wake up and look at all of the magnificent things around you. Stop being a scared victim, and start being a brave victor. It's time to take back your power. That's right, I said it. You are a powerful badass. It's time for you to find your peace again.

One of the first ways to find peace and to find your power again is to change your attitude and mindset surrounding your situation. Try not to see divorce as a death sentence. Don't keep asking yourself, "Why did this happen to me?" I used to say, "This isn't fair. Other people have happy families. Why can't I?" You need to get out of that victim mentality and quickly. You also need to stop comparing yourself to others.

Be grateful for all of the wonderful things you do have. Gratitude attracts more of the positive things we want in life. Try to look at this as a new beginning. Try to see it as an adventure and a chance to experience something new.

New Beginnings

Remember the hand coming down to slap you? This happened to you for a reason, so ask yourself, "What was I supposed to learn from this?" If you really think about it, there was probably an obvious lesson there like standing up for yourself.

New beginnings can be scary but they can also be very thrilling. The beginning of something new is a positive thing. One of my favorite times of year as a teacher is the first day of school. Everyone is filled with excitement. Students are eager to meet you. They don't have any expectations. I have an opportunity to really make a connection with them. If I feel there were things that I could have done better than last year, I have the chance to fix them. The same thing applies to you and your life. It's never too late to make a fresh start.

A new beginning means you have a clean slate and a new opportunity to be who you were destined to be. You can be the best possible version of yourself, so it's time to figure out what the best version of you looks like.

Besides, nothing will piss off your ex more than your finding success and being happy. That will really irritate him, which is just a bonus. You're smiling now, aren't you?

～

Positive Thinking

Maybe you are not the type of person who is a positive thinker, and I get that. Maybe you are thinking, *I'm not a touchy-feely person, so this is not for me.* I was more prone to be negative, and I played the victim for a long time too. The problem with this is that it doesn't get you anywhere, and it is miserable—I mean seriously miserable—and everyone will think that you are a bummer. You will look like Eeyore with your constant complaining, tail falling off, and that perpetual rain cloud above your head.

Plus, thinking negative thoughts lowers your energy vibration, which can cause all kinds of things to happen. You can become physically sick, you can unintentionally attract people who are negative into your life, and the list goes on.

Do you really want that? I didn't think so. So, how do you avoid that? You can start by being more positive.

Positive thinking is essential, especially because, believe it or not, what we think is what we create. You are creating your own private hell with your negative thoughts. When we constantly worry and have fears and doubts, we are sending a message out to the Universe that these are the things we want to manifest.

I sincerely doubt that you want negative things to

continue to happen to you. If you do, then you need to go see a professional. There is something seriously wrong with you. I'm only kidding.

Really, though, in order to ensure that you are not attracting negative things into your life, you have to change how and what you are thinking. This is not an especially easy task if you have had a particular mindset your whole life, but you can retrain your brain to think and respond differently. You absolutely have to do that.

Here is another thing to think about... When we are angry and upset with other people, we aren't making them suffer. We are making ourselves suffer. As much as you want your ex to feel the death rays that you are privately sending him, he isn't feeling a thing. Our exes don't hear our thoughts about them or know that we wish them a slow and painful death. They don't care. They have moved on. They are so over it already. We are the ones who will suffer. You are allowing your ex to live rent-free in your head. Do you really want that?

Your best revenge is to move on and be happy. You deserve to live your best life possible. Is that really going to be a life where you are in a bad mood, constantly plotting revenge, wondering what your ex is currently doing or being depressed all of the time? I don't think so. Snap out of it, sister. Start thinking about all of the awesome things in life that you deserve and that you are going to receive. Something else to think about is that you never see a happy ending on the true crime television show *Snapped*.

Tapping

It may feel like trying to change your thoughts and attitude is like trying to herd cats, but don't give up. The good news is that there are a lot of resources out there to help you get rid of your negative thought patterns. One way is through Emotional Freedom Techniques or EFT. EFT is a psychological tool that is used to "tap" out the emotions that you are feeling that no longer serve you.

We are often blocked from experiencing our true potential because of past traumas. In this case, your past trauma is your divorce, but you may even be carrying around stuff from your childhood or even a past life. EFT is a way to release our bodies of those traumas.

Remember that we retain our memories at the cellular level, which means our bodies are holding on to things that our conscious minds no longer remember.

There are many free YouTube videos for practicing

EFT. Each video is specifically designed for different emotions or situations that you are going through. Julia Treat has many of these videos on her YouTube channel. Brad Yates and Nick Ortner also post some great EFT videos on YouTube. They are all amazing.

You can do these anytime, and they don't take very long. The videos are anywhere from three minutes to eight minutes in length. It's a very manageable chunk of time. You can do them as many times as you need to do them.

As soon as you start to feel those negative thoughts creeping in, take time out to tap. It's really a way of talking out those emotions that no longer serve us and getting rid of them at the cellular level. This may seem strange to you at first if you have never done it, but it works. You can even do them in the car while driving to work.

Sometimes on my long drive home, I start to feel anxious. I'm an overthinker from way back, so it's something I do quite well. I overanalyze past relationships or something that happened to me during my day. Now, when I start to feel myself doing that, I stop myself and do a tapping exercise. I feel better immediately. They're super easy, so you have no excuse not to do them.

∼

PEP TALKS

It is super important that we keep our thoughts positive, so another great thing that you can do every day is to repeat a mantra to yourself. Think of it as giving yourself a pep talk. We all need those from time to time, but,unfortunately, when you get older, no one gives them to you anymore. Some of us never got them in the first place. That's probably part of our problem. I blame moms.

The awesome thing is that you can give yourself the pep talk you deserve. This may seem strange if you aren't used to doing this, but it will do wonders for your self-confidence, and, no, you will not look like Stuart Smalley from *Saturday Night Live* either, but you are good enough, smart enough... You get the drill.

Just do this first thing in the morning as you are getting ready for work or to start your day. There are many good resources out there that are free where you can find mantras. Just search online for mantras, find the one that resonates with you, and get started. Think about what you need to hear the most and use a mantra that addresses that. Look at yourself in the mirror every day and repeat your favorite mantra. I personally like to tell myself each day that I love myself deeply, completely, and unconditionally. I tell myself that it is safe to be me.

Also, because I was hurt in the past, I throw in that it is safe to love and to be loved unconditionally and that I am letting go of unhealthy attachments and relationships in my life.

No, I'm not a narcissist (stop judging me ... you don't know me), and you aren't being one either. Remember, you have to believe that you love yourself. This is a major step in the healing process.

~

STILL THE MIND

Meditation is probably the most constructive thing you can do for yourself, and it is the easiest. Even if you think that you will not be able to meditate because you have ADD, and your mind will wander, and that sale ends tomorrow, you have to pick up the kids at four, you need to switch your laundry over from the washer to the dryer ... believe me, I understand.

My mind tends to wander as well. It's amazing all of the crazy ideas that will pop into your head when you are trying to quiet it, like why don't pizza tacos exist? They are the two greatest foods melded into one. We already have taco pizzas, so why not pizza tacos? Maybe they do exist, I just haven't had one yet.

I wonder where I could get one. Ugh, you see what I mean?

Not to worry, steady practice will help you to work past that. Start off small with short meditations. You can do them in the morning or before bed. If you are a subscriber to my podcast "Awaken Your Inner Awesomeness" then you will already know that I have meditations available for free. If you are not a subscriber, then get with it and subscribe already, sister. I'm just kidding. I do have a lot of other great resources on my podcast. Feel free to check it out.

You can also subscribe to my website www.melissaoatman.com and receive a free morning and evening meditation. Julia Treat also has a really good morning and evening meditation that you can get on her website. They are free. You can do them anytime you have a chance to find a quiet, comfortable place. Many people falsely believe that you have to lie down to meditate. This is not true at all. You simply need to be comfortable and be able to close your eyes, so no meditating while driving—please!

Actually, you can listen to meditations while you drive, just no closing those eyes. You can still benefit from what you hear. It's best, though, in order to get the full benefits of meditation, if you can find a nice quiet, comfortable place to close your eyes and relax.

Getting into the habit of practicing meditation will help you shift your energy vibration to higher levels, which in turn will make you feel better. Also, a regular meditation practice can help you to strengthen your intuition.

Medically speaking, meditation has many wonderful health benefits, such as lowering blood pressure, reducing anxiety and depression, improving sleep, and reducing or controlling pain. It definitely has emotional benefits as well. It can help us to become more focused in our daily lives. You can also get in touch with your higher self and discover your life's purpose. Knowing what our life's purpose can help us in all areas of our lives, like finding our dream job —you know; the one where you never have to work a day in your life.

There are many different topics for meditations, such as finding peace, releasing fear, losing weight, or finding your soul mate. Choose a meditation to fit the area that you want to work on the most. There are many free meditations out there on YouTube. There are also free apps that offer mediations.

The important thing is to find the ones that resonate with you. If you don't like the sound of the speaker's voice, it might be difficult to relax. If you don't like the terms they use in the meditation, then move on to something else. Find a few that you like and that you find relaxing. There are so many out there that you don't need to try to stick with one you don't like. Even if you fall asleep during the meditation, that is OK. It will still benefit you.

There are even meditations that are actually designed for you to do while you are sleeping. I have never personally tried those, but feel free to give it a shot if you think it would help. Starting and ending your day with meditation (it only takes five minutes) is a great way to shift your energy. It will make your day more positive, give you more peaceful sleep at night, and you will attract more of the things you want into your life.

MUSIC

Music also does wonders for our soul. Listening to uplifting music is something that is so easy to do, yet it is often overlooked. We know that we can drown our sorrows by listening to sad songs, but you probably never thought about elevating your mood by listening to uplifting music. It does work though.

We have no doubt all listened to sad songs after a breakup. I understand doing that at first because you do have to get your emotions out, but why on earth would you want to stay depressed? So, go ahead and listen to a few sad songs, cry your eyes out, and then snap the hell out of it. What are you trying to do ... be a total bummer?

Don't spend all of your time dwelling on the past. That is so pointless and will do you no good. The only thing you are going to accomplish is to increase your sadness and make yourself miserable.

There is a saying that goes, "If you are depressed, you are living in the past. If you are anxious, you are living in the future. If you have peace, then you are living in the present."

This is so true. Try not to dwell in the past because that will set you back in your progress and lower your energy vibration. We already talked about what happens when you do that. Instead, listen to some fun, uplifting songs, sing along, dance, and go crazy. This will raise your energy and make you feel good. Isn't that what you wanted? If not, why did you buy this book?

I can't help you if you insist on being a total downer. It's easy to listen to soothing or happy music. There's even a song called "Happy." I mean what more do you want? You probably listen to uplifting music anyway, so why not do it more often?

You can listen while cleaning, going for a walk, taking a relaxing bath, or driving—if you do it while driving, don't go too crazy with your dancing or you may have an accident and that would not be good ... people might also start giving you weird looks. Well, just forget those people, they suck! How rude staring like that. Listen to your music and dance like no one is watching. You are a dancing queen.

Podcasts

Podcasts are another tool that you can use to help you heal. There are some great podcasts out there that offer advice and words of wisdom. Not to brag or anything, but I know of a great podcast called "Awaken Your Inner Awesomeness". That girl who does that podcast is amazing. She's totally cool, funny, and is an all-around badass. You will love her.

You can listen to uplifting podcasts on the way to work or when you are out running errands. I have a long commute to and from my job, so I have plenty of time to kill. I used to listen to music, which is also good, but there are many powerful and informative podcasts that can help encourage and support you.

One of the podcasts that I stumbled upon that really gave me hope is "Stepping into the Light." It's amazing what you can learn from other people; just look how much you are learning from me ... aren't you lucky?

There are many topics out there that you can choose from. I would recommend finding a podcast that inspires you and gives you some daily wisdom. In the mornings, it will motivate you, and in the evenings it can help you relax and unwind.

Many comedians have podcasts too. Sometimes it is just good to laugh. It melts away all of the day's stress. Ask your friends to recommend some good podcasts (but not Karen, who knows what she listens to). You will probably get some great ideas (Karen will probably not give you any good ideas. Avoid her). You can even learn a new language through podcasts. Look at you. You are going to be so sophisticated ... ooh la la.

~

Social Media

One other simple thing that you can do for yourself is to avoid social media. That got your attention, didn't it? OK, so you don't have to necessarily avoid it, but you should watch what you are devoting your time to on social media. Social media sites are great because they can help keep us connected to family and friends whom we may not see often.

The problem with social media, though, is that it can be a source of great negativity. Think about what people post. Are they constantly posting about beautiful things or are they complaining?

Chances are you have someone or a few someones that you can think of right now who constantly gripe about everything on social media (that'd be Karen). We all know those Debbie Downers (or Karen Killjoys). They post everything from "the world is going to end tomorrow" to videos of animal abuse (seriously, Karen? No one wanted to see that. NO ONE!).

You need to try to unfollow those people if at all possible. They won't realize that you aren't following them, so you will not be hurting feelings. You will be saving your own sanity.

Constantly surrounding yourself with negative people is only going to drag you down to their level. We already drag ourselves down enough. We don't need anyone else to do that for us. Instead, you should be around people whose energies are higher than yours because they will pull you up to their level.

We also tend to get our news from social media, which can be an additional source of frustration. What we see can be so negative and heartbreaking.

People's behavior on social media has become abhorrent. They will resort to name calling over topics with which they disagree. A lot of bullying goes on through social media, which may make you angry or frustrated. This will drain you of your energy for sure.

The overarching theme of our news is death and disaster. The media industry thrives on bad news because it sells. It can be very challenging to avoid reading negative stories. This can stress you out and cause your blood pressure to go up. Instead of always feeding into the negative news stories, try to ensure that you are seeing mostly positive influences on social media.

This can be difficult, but there are things you can do to ensure that you aren't being bogged down by negativity. I already suggested that you unfollow people who are constant complainers. You will feel lighter and good riddance (Bye, Karen). Yikes, people can be bummers.

The other thing you can do is to limit the news feeds you subscribe to. Once you have limited those things, you should subscribe to more positive groups and feeds. I like to subscribe to pages that offer daily wisdom or positive quotes. There are also sites that offer daily tarot card readings for free, which I find gives me a sense of direction for the day or week.

I also subscribe to groups like a single mom's group. Like-minded groups can help you feel supported, and you can get some good advice as well. The positive feeds will lift up your spirits and help you to raise your vibration, which I already said makes you feel good. It won't bring you down like the other aforementioned forms of social media will.

One more thing to consider is that when we constantly see other people's awesome lives on Facebook or Instagram, we tend to compare ourselves to them. "Why is Karen in Hawaii? That is **my** dream vacation." "How is **Karen** able to afford that huge house? She works at the gas station." We can also experience FOMO, or fear of missing out. "Why didn't Karen invite **me** to her pool party? I can't believe she invited everyone **except** me. I wonder if someone told her I wrote some mean things about her?"

Anyway, I already talked about how comparing ourselves to others is not good for our self-esteem. You can see now why it is so easy to do. If it is at all possible, you may want to take breaks now and then from social media. I know that's asking a lot because you probably don't even realize just how much you rely on social media; however, taking a break may help you put things into perspective.

Be grateful for all of the awesome things that you have, and don't be jealous of the things that you perceive that others have. Having an attitude of gratitude will do wonders for you.

Cutting Cords from the Past

Another tool that most people really don't think about or even know about is past life regression. Many religions teach that we are only here once; so many people don't even give this a second thought. While I respect other religions, I really do believe that we have been here more than one time and that we carry with us some of the emotional baggage from previous experiences.

One of my mentors always says that our past lives run the show for most of us. Many of us are still carrying emotional baggage from our childhoods, so you can imagine how much baggage you are carrying around if you consider that you've had many lives. I'm picturing a poor bellboy carrying bags around his neck and in each arm. Those bags get heavy, and they are part of what is blocking us from living our best lives here. So, what can you do about it? If you think that there is nothing you can do about it, then you are wrong ... so there! Take that, Karen! You are wrong!

One specific thing you can do to get rid of some of

this baggage is to meditate. There are meditation exercises that take you to your past lives and allow you to see exactly what lessons you were meant to learn. You can then ask to be healed of the things you brought with you into this lifetime.

For example, let's imagine that in a past life you never asked others for help and struggled to make ends meet, so you died an early death due to fatigue because you worked too much. You could see that the lesson here might be to learn to ask for help. You could then use that lesson in this life.

Are you repeating the same behavior? Do you still struggle to ask others for help? Sometimes we do keep repeating the same patterns of behavior in each lifetime. These are karmic lessons that we need to learn. Until we learn them, we keep revisiting them.

You can also ask the angels and your spiritual team to give you what you needed but did not have in your past life. In this case, you could ask the angels to assist you in learning how to ask for help when you need it. This is just one example of a possible past life lesson. Each person has his or her own lessons to learn. You may have several lessons that you are bringing with you from past lives.

There are many great meditations out there for learning about your past lives. If you are new to meditation, or you try the meditations but aren't getting results, you can also seek a professional to help you. Just make sure you do your research and find someone reputable. The lessons that we came here to learn have to be learned in one life or another. Why not make it this life?

Another great tool is a cord-cutting exercise. You can ask Archangel Michael to come in and cut the negative energetic cords that are tying you to people or situations that are no longer serving you. There are some excellent cord-cutting meditations on YouTube. I also have a free cord-cutting meditation on my podcast.

When we visualize Archangel Michael taking his sword of healing light and cutting away those cords, we are freeing ourselves of the heavy burdens we carry that are associated with those cords. You will feel so much better and lighter afterwards.

REIKI

If you are feeling totally stuck and as though you can't move past your emotional wounds, you might want to seek professional help. A great holistic medical tool that you can try is Reiki.

Reiki is an ancient Japanese healing technique. The belief is that you can restore someone's physical and emotional well-being through energy. We are all made of energy, so if part of your energy becomes depleted (usually through emotional trauma), you can restore that energy through Reiki.

Reiki uses life flow energy, which is channeled to the person in need of healing. Many physical ailments come about because a person is dealing with something emotional on a deeper level. I truly believe that most of our diseases, illnesses, and physical pain come from unresolved emotional issues.

We have seven energy chakra centers in our body. They are each aligned to different organs and functions in our body. If any one of these chakras becomes blocked, then you will experience a physical or emotional symptom. Reiki is a great way to feel emotionally and physically restored, and during a Reiki session, your chakras can be opened and unblocked.

Hope is something that is so important, yet we tend to lose it in times of tragedy. You really need to have hope because your future is going to be so magnificent. Even if you can't see that now, I promise you that you are headed for great things.

One way to help you sustain hope is to create a vision board. This is not only a fun thing to do, but it will also give a glimpse into the future you so sincerely deserve. What do you want your life to look like? What kind of job do you want? What do you want your home to look like?

Sometimes we don't even know the answers to these questions ourselves. It's fun to daydream about having a cool life. Most of us do it all of the time, so why not make your daydreams useful? Start thinking about how you want to see yourself.

Don't worry about how others see you or how you might receive the things you want. Focus on you and what you want. What would make you happy?

Start adding pictures of all of the things you wish to attract on your vision board. If you are an artistic person, you could make your vision board a physical one where you paste pictures or draw pictures of the things you desire.

If you are like me and can't draw a stick figure with a ruler and a pencil, you could use a program like Pinterest to create your board. It doesn't really matter how you create it. What matters is that you include all of the things you wish to attract, like money, health, a job, a house, a spouse, you get the picture.

Make sure that you look at that board every day for at least a minute or two. Visualize what it would look like to have those things. What would it feel like if all of your dreams came true? Get a sense of that. Feel the joy in your bones. You are telling the Universe that you want these things and that you are ready to receive them.

It's important that you don't worry about how you will receive the things listed on your vision board because the Universe has very unique and clever ways of sending us gifts. Now, sit back and get ready for the abundance.

~

LIMITING BELIEFS

A limiting belief is a belief that we hold about some topic that is not true and holds us back. Most people have beliefs that were taught to them as children or that they picked up from society.

These beliefs can be about money, love, religion, or even your own self-worth. They can also be very damaging. Many of the beliefs we hold are actually holding us back from experiencing life to the fullest.

Here is a list of some common limiting beliefs about money:

- I have to work hard to earn money.
- I am barely getting by.
- There is always just enough.
- Money is the root of all evil.

- Money isn't important.
- I'm not good with money.
- The rich get richer and the poor get poorer.

One of the most common limiting beliefs about money is that it is bad to want it. It is absolutely OK to want money. We have to have money to eat, to live, basically for everything. Why shouldn't we want it?

Another common belief is that you have to work hard to earn money. If you keep telling yourself that you have to work hard for your money, then you will. You don't have to work your fingers to the bone to earn money. That's just a limiting belief that you have heard all of your life.

These beliefs are keeping you from receiving the money you so richly deserve. That's right ... I said you deserve to be rich. You do deserve it; in fact, we all do.

There is nothing wrong with wanting to be successful or having a financially comfortable life-style. It doesn't make you greedy or evil. We need money in order to survive. We need money in order to support our favorite charities. Money serves our highest good. Why would we limit ourselves?

It's nice to have nice things. That doesn't make us bad people. Money does not have negative energy. It is neutral. We are the ones who give it a negative value. This is a hard one for some people to let go of, but you have to let that go. Quit limiting your ability to make money. Don't you want all of the things on your vision board? It's going to take money for that, so you are going to need to change your attitude about money.

Love is another area where we have limiting beliefs. Do any of these sound familiar?

- I don't deserve love.
- Dating is scary.
- I have to find someone by a certain time.
- I'm too old to find love again.
- There are no good people out there/All the good ones are taken.
- I'm afraid he/she will leave.
- I'm not good enough/pretty enough/skinny enough.
- True love is hard to find.

It is sad that so many of us feel that we are unworthy of love or that love is so hard to find. These are all too common beliefs held by many. These beliefs will surely block love from finding you.

Many of us are so afraid of being hurt again that we put up armor around our heart and guard it like it was a vault full of money. I know that you want to find love again. In order to do that, you have to learn to let go of these beliefs, which are really just lies that we tell ourselves. We've heard these lies so many times that we believe they are actually true. They are not. They are simply things that we have heard so often that we believe they are true.

You deserve to find the love of your life, and there isn't necessarily just one. You can have many great loves in your lifetime if you so choose. Stop telling yourself that there is only one mister right or one soul mate or that you missed him. That simply isn't true.

The final limiting belief category is about how we see ourselves or our self-worth. This one is so sad because it shows that we see ourselves as less than we are or unworthy. Ask yourself whether you have ever had these thoughts before:

- I can't do this.
- I'm not smart enough.
- I'm not talented enough.
- I'm not good enough.
- I don't deserve success.

This surely makes God and the Universe sad. We were wonderfully and beautifully made. We are all just love, but we seem to forget that. We give in to fear and let it overtake our thoughts and emotions. Fear is just an illusion. Only love is real. We forget how awesome God thinks we are. He loves us so much and wants only the best for us, so why do we continue to doubt that?

Our ego has a lot to do with that. What is this ego, and what does it have to do with our limiting beliefs? According to the dictionary, ego is defined as the part of the mind that mediates between the conscious and the unconscious and is responsible for reality testing and a sense of personal identity. What that essentially means is that the ego is the part of our brain that takes over and sends us those lovely messages like, "You aren't good enough." Don't you just love the ego? Reminds me of Karen.

Know this... You are powerful, capable, and loved. You can do whatever you put your energy toward, but you have to believe in yourself. You can't let that ego take over. Next time your ego wants to butt in, put a gag in its mouth.

How can we get all of the things we so richly deserve? This is where your vision board can help.

Look at all of the things you said you wanted and believe that you deserve them. Trust that you will receive them. Feel what it would be like to have them.

What I want you to do after you have had a chance to identify and study your limiting beliefs is get rid of them. We can do that symbolically by burning our lists (just do it in a contained manner and don't set your house on fire) or tearing them up. Look at them and think to yourself, *You are not holding me back anymore. I believe the opposite of these things now. You are just lies that I have told myself. From now on, I am going to start telling myself only facts.* Then either burn or tear up your list and every time you start to tell yourself one of those lies, stop yourself and replace it with the truth.

You can also do meditations and tapping exercises to rid yourself of those pesky beliefs. Just this morning, I was thinking about writing this book and wondering if it would actually help anyone. I knew this was a limiting belief rearing its ugly head, so I did a tapping exercise in the car. I felt much better afterwards. I felt brave enough to start writing more of my story. So, I can tell you with confidence that these tools work because I use them every day myself.

~

Guilt

In addition to our limiting beliefs, many divorced people deal with guilt. Guilt will hold you back from finding peace for sure. Whether you feel guilt over things that happened in your marriage that led to the divorce, the divorce itself, or the effect that the divorce is having on your kids, one thing is certain—you need to let it go.

Just imagine yourself singing that song from *Frozen* at the top of your lungs. Did you embarrass your kids? Good, that is your job. You have to let that stuff go. You can't find peace again until you can let go of any guilty feelings that you are experiencing that are associated with the divorce. It is not serving you at all.

There is nothing positive that guilt is going to do for you. You are not going to earn your spot in heaven by being a martyr. You are simply beating yourself up, which does exactly what it sounds like. It makes you feel like shit. You are playing the victim, which makes you weak. You are not a victim. You can control what happens to you.

If you are feeling guilty because of others (we all have those people in our lives who try to give us advice, but really they just want us to feel guilty. Karen is really the worst), then you need to think about distancing yourself from them or asking them to stop trying to make you feel bad. Basically, tell them to mind their own damn business. That means you, Karen.

❧

Boundaries

Maybe you are having these issues with people because you don't know how to properly set boundaries with them. That is something that many of us struggle with as adults. We never learned how to do that as children.

There are wonderful books out there about setting healthy boundaries that are very useful. Stand your ground and do not let others make you feel less awesome than you are. We already do that to ourselves as it is.

Use the techniques mentioned above to let go of any guilt that you feel. Remember that a rear-view mirror is small for a reason. We shouldn't spend the majority of our lives looking back at what was. It just fills us with regret and anxiety. Instead, live fully in the moments that you do have and look forward to the future roads that lie ahead.

If you devote the time to working on yourself, you will find your peace again. You will sleep through the night without crying yourself to sleep, you won't want to curl up in a ball on the couch, and you will look forward to tomorrow. It's all going to be OK, and you are going to be great. I know this for a fact. I am living proof.

You have to do the work in order to see the work in

you. This can seem overwhelming, I know, but start by taking small steps. Start by adding one meditation before bed; then, when you are ready, add one in the morning.

Tell yourself at least once a day that you love yourself (and believe it!), and then you can do it twice a day. Make a list of all of the wonderful qualities that you have. You have a lot to offer this world. Do something nice for yourself like schedule a massage or take a hot bath. When you feel those insecurities rearing their ugly heads, stop and do a tapping exercise or meditate. You have all of the tools that you need right at your fingertips, and almost all of them are free.

You always care for others and now you deserve to be cared for too and who knows better how to care for you than you? You are worth the effort you are spending to make your life better, and it is going to be amazing!

JOURNALING MOMENT

TALENTS

Are you using your gifts and talents fully? Everyone has a gift. What is yours?

Write down any talents you feel you have in your journal. Are you utilizing those talents?

If there weren't any specific talents that were obvious to you, then think about what you enjoy doing. Is there anything that you really have a passion for? Do you like to sing? Do you like to paint? Do you like talking to people?

You may be talented in an area that you never realized could be useful. Think about all of your interests and begin writing them down. Maybe you are interested in something that you've never tried before. List those things as well, and then, when possible, try to do those activities.

If you were interested in playing piano but never did, why not sign up for lessons? You may discover a new passion hidden deep within you. It's never too late for self-discovery. True happiness comes from doing what you love and have a passion for. What will make you feel truly fulfilled?

JOURNALING MOMENT

WRITE OUT YOUR FEELINGS

In addition to meditation, writing in your journal is a great way to get out your feelings. You may not even know what it is you are feeling.

Many times, I am feeling yucky, but I won't know why. I sit down and write in my journal and think about my day. It will suddenly become apparent that there is a very clear reason why I am feeling the way I am. I just had to write about it.

You can write every day or just a few times a week. It's totally up to you. I would journal how you are feeling each day. It's a beneficial way to release those emotions that are no longer serving you.

Furthermore, it would be interesting to see how your writing changes as you move through the healing process. You may see that your writings were sad and melancholy at first, but then they change to hopeful and joyful. You will surely see how far you have come.

List Limiting Beliefs

Another thing that I would suggest you write in your journal is any limiting belief that you have.

6

FALLING BACK INTO OLD PATTERNS

OR HOW NOT TO KEEP SCREWING UP OVER AND OVER
AGAIN

*B*eing a single parent can be an overwhelming experience. It could be easy to long for the old days when you had a partner around to help you. I'm sure life was easier for you then, and that is perfectly understandable. It's normal to wish that life were simpler. We all tend to look back at the past with rose-colored glasses.

In fact, I remember a time when I was trying to get over an ex, and out of the blue he texted me to see how I was doing. I, of course, took this as a sign from the Universe that he loved me, missed me, and regretted letting me go because I'm such an awesome person and a fantastic catch, and he realized what a colossal mistake he had made.

Have you ever been there before? I'm pretty sure you have. I'm also pretty positive that this wasn't really the case at all. I'm fairly certain he just wanted to make sure I hadn't killed myself because I was so devastated that he broke up with me. Yes, he had the ego that ate New York. I'm kidding of course. No relationship is worth ending your life over.

Seriously, though, my point (I almost forgot what it was) is that when I received this text, it sent me into a tailspin. I started thinking about all of the great times we had and how much I missed him, and I experienced a lot of regret for not trying harder to make that relationship work.

Then I snapped back to reality. What I was forcing myself not to remember was that the entire time I was with him he made me feel insecure. I totally forgot about the jerkish (is that a word? Google thinks it's a word... I guess it's a word) things he had done to me. When I really sat and thought about it, I had been relieved when we broke up.

Even though we did have a lot of good times, there were things that he had done to me that were really awful. Like "what kind of a person would do that to another human being" kind of awful. Well, they weren't really that bad, but I would never allow myself to be treated that way today.

Did I really miss that? No, I did not. However, I could easily see how someone could forget about all of the bad things and only focus on the good times.

Indeed, it is extremely easy to only remember the good.

LIFE LESSONS

There is a very logical reason why we only tend to remember the good parts about our past relationships, and that is because our brain has a built-in mechanism to block out past hurts. What that means is that in order to protect us from our own memories, we tend to bury the things that hurt us deep down inside. That way they can't hurt us anymore.

The problem with that is that those memories and feelings didn't really go away. They are still there, and they will rear their ugly heads at some point. We usually end up projecting those hurt feelings onto someone else, and they can end up wreaking havoc on our future relationships.

I truly believe that if you don't heal your past, you will bleed all over people who didn't cut you. What you need to realize is that it can be easy to want to fall back into old patterns and to have a strong desire to get back together with an ex, but I strongly advise against this. There were obviously reasons why this relationship did not work. I would assume that they were very serious reasons as well. So, what were they?

There is something else to consider. There were most likely lessons that you had to learn with this partner. If you recall the chapter about finding peace when I talked about forgiveness, we come here to work with others to learn difficult life lessons.

It's possible that you and your ex agreed to come here and experience this relationship in order for you to learn and for your soul to grow. So, what were your lessons, and did you learn them? If you go back to an ex simply because it is too difficult to do things on your own, you may be delaying your own spiritual growth. You are also delaying meeting the perfect soul mate for you.

One thing that I have discovered is that you can't avoid learning a lesson. If you don't learn it now, you will have to learn it at some point. In reuniting with an ex, you are probably just prolonging the lesson that you were meant to learn. You are better off learning it sooner rather than later.

I know what you are thinking though. You are probably thinking that it does work out for some people. You are correct. It does sometimes work out for some people. That doesn't mean that they didn't have to learn a lesson first. You've probably also heard of many people who get back together with an ex only to break up again a few years later. They probably just delayed the lesson that they were supposed to learn. I will stress that this isn't always the case, but it definitely is a common occurrence. I don't believe that this is just a coincidence.

As I said earlier, there were reasons why this relationship did not work out, and they must have been significant enough for you to go through the process of divorce because no one would want to go through that mess unless it was absolutely necessary. I urge you to think about what it is that you were supposed to learn from this relationship. It could be that you were simply supposed to learn how to walk away from something that no longer served you.

As uncomplicated as that may sound, it is a serious lesson for a lot of people and can be extremely difficult to do. We try so hard to hang on to things that aren't really helping us grow spiritually. I know that I had a major issue with this.

I stayed in relationships for far too long simply because I didn't want to hurt someone else's feelings. I know that seems really silly, yet this is the pattern that I kept repeating. I also did not speak up for myself in relationships and gave more than I got. I was a people pleaser.

I finally realized that this wasn't serving me at all, and so I made the decision to change the way I acted in relationships. I had to learn that I can't change how other people behave, but I can change how I behave. I wasted a lot of time that I could have spent being available for the right person by continuing to be with the wrong one or hoping to reunite with the wrong one.

~

Suppressed Feelings

I mentioned earlier that we often suppress feelings in order to protect ourselves. Researchers at Stanford University found that the human brain actually has a biological mechanism for suppressing painful memories. That's right ... our brains are trying to protect us from the bad stuff.

While this may seem like a positive thing, in fact, it is preventing us from healing from those painful memories. So, although it is trying to help us, our brain is actually hindering our spiritual growth. That's right, I said it ... our brain is hurting us.

We absolutely need to heal the pain caused by those memories. Remember that those emotions are still there. They haven't gone away. We just don't remember them. If we do not heal the emotional pain, we could do things in our future relationships that are unhealthy because of our past hurts.

This can in turn cause us to sabotage future relationships. It's almost like I have done that before or something. "So, how are you supposed to heal those memories?" I'm so glad you asked because there are a few things that you can do to heal.

Many of the tools I mentioned in Chapter 5 (Finding Peace) can assist you in the healing process. So, if you are already using those tools, then you are probably at present healing yourself even as we speak. If you are doing this, way to go. You are doing an awesome job. Remember to be patient because it is a process. You may not feel better right away, but I promise that you will feel better. If you haven't started using those tools yet, don't worry. You can start using them at any time.

~

FORGIVENESS

One of the ideas mentioned in Chapter 4 was forgiveness. I talked about how important it is to forgive those who have hurt us, and that includes your ex. What I failed to mention is that forgiving yourself is even more crucial.

We often think about forgiveness as something we give other people, yet we forget that we need to forgive ourselves as well. We are probably harder on ourselves than anyone else ever could be, so it is important to give yourself some slack.

Forgiveness can be a very healing thing. You are an awesome person who deserves a lot of love, and forgiveness is a way of loving ourselves. You are worthy of it, and it will renew your spirit. You can totally use the radical forgiveness sheets on yourself as well. You will be amazed at how much better and lighter you feel once you have forgiven yourself.

Change

Change is never an easy thing. As human beings, we naturally resist change as much as possible. It is so uncomfortable to be pushed out of our comfort zones, but if you really sat down and thought about it, you would see that this is necessary for us to grow.

If we were allowed to, we would do the same thing day in and day out simply because it's easy and comfortable. There is a quote that I love. Most people attribute this quote to Albert Einstein (I'm not sure that he actually said it, but I really think that it is awesome). It says, "Insanity is doing the same thing over and over again and expecting different results." This quote is spot on, and, no, I am not calling you crazy.

However, I do find it interesting that we act the same way in each relationship we have, yet we expect different results. It is certainly something to think about. So, I would venture to say that the moral of this chapter is that if you want your relationships to be better, you have to change your behavior in them.

Heal your emotional baggage, and leave those exes behind you. They're just slowing you down from receiving all of the awesome stuff that the Universe thinks you deserve. Don't forget that you could be opening yourself up to receive someone even better than your ex.

Did you ever stop to think that your next husband could have all of the looks of Ryan Gosling, the charm of Ryan Reynolds, and bankroll of Elon Musk? You get the picture. This new guy will probably make your ex seem like a loser … like a totally pathetic loser, which he totally is for breaking your heart. What a jerk!

JOURNALING MOMENT

FIX IT

Take a moment to write in your journal and list the things that made you unhappy in your relationship.

Could those things really go away? Are those things that you can fix? Is your ex-partner even willing to fix it? What needs do you have? Is your partner willing or able to provide for those needs?

If you said no to any of those things, then you are truly better off allowing your ex to remain an ex.

JOURNALING MOMENT

LESSONS

It's important to reflect on what wasn't working in your relationship. That is where we usually find the lessons. I want you to take some time to reflect.

Write in your journal about the issues you had in your relationship. The lesson that you were supposed to learn with this relationship may become apparent to you through your journaling.

If it is still not obvious to you what you were supposed to learn from this failed relationship (and please do not misunderstand me, you are not a failure), then you can do some meditations. We can ask our higher selves what lesson(s) we were supposed to learn. You can do that through a guided meditation.

Those meditations can be found on YouTube by

searching for the key words *higher self* and *learning*. You can also ask your angels and spiritual guides to help you understand what lessons you were supposed to learn.

Be mindful that you must be patient and open for the answer. It may require sitting in stillness for a few moments in order to hear the guidance. The sooner you learn the lessons that this relationship brought, the sooner you can get on with your life and move forward. You will probably notice that your future relationships improve as well.

7

MY EX IS DATING AGAIN,

AND I WANT TO KILL MYSELF

*E*ventually, both you and your ex are going to move on to other partners. The problem comes when your ex moves on first. This could be a shock to you. It may hurt to see your ex with someone new, or it may downright piss you off. I mean this ass was really a jerk to you, and now he's happy again with someone else. The absolute nerve of him! It isn't fair, is it?

Well, guess what? It's totally fair. That was your ego talking, and your ego is an ungracious ass. Your ego needs to be taken down a peg or two. You are allowing yourself to fall into victimhood when you say things like, "It isn't fair."

It may hurt or sting to see your ex happy with someone else and it may feel unfair that you don't have someone else or that it didn't work out with you, but that is simply fear getting the best of you. It's also your ego because it is embarrassing or hurtful when someone moves on from you. That person vowed to love you until death, so it's only fair that he should have to curl up and die without you, right?

Look, this can be a very tricky subject, and I have been there. Believe me. I used to say it wasn't fair all of the time. I didn't date for a long time after my divorce in order to focus on the kids, and my ex moved on with no problems. That made me very angry at first because I felt that it was unfair. I was doing all of the heavy lifting, and he led a carefree life. He could go out whenever he pleased.

The thing is that I chose to live that life. It was my choice not to date and to focus on my kids. Looking back, I realize that I could have made time for dating. I was probably avoiding it for fear of getting hurt again. I was spending so much time playing the victim that I got stuck there. It wasn't fun at all.

My point is that you have to let go of that stuff. What your ex does in his personal life is now none of your business. Repeat after me, "What your ex does in his personal life is none of your business." Just as whatever you do in your personal life is now none of his business. It's so important for you to make that distinction and to set that boundary.

What you are really dealing with is the fact that you still have emotional baggage that you need to let go of. So, you may want to grab some Kleenex and a carton of ice cream for this chapter because we are going to dig deep.

If you have children, you can't move on and have a normal parental relationship with your ex if you resent him or his new partner, especially if he ends up marrying someone else. This person will be the stepmom to your children, and I know you want to be able to get along with this person because of your kids.

That's going to be tough to do if you are bitter and angry. Are you on the couch sobbing again? I am so sorry. I know this is a painful subject, but it is so necessary in order to heal and move on. You don't want to look like the crazy ex, do you?

Let's start by looking at what this is really about. Is it about your ex forgetting you and moving on or is it about you feeling abandoned or not feeling like a whole person yet? Are you constantly thinking about your ex?

The tricky thing is that we all have different opinions about our exes after a divorce. Some may be doing a dance of victory that they got rid of him, while others may be pining away wishing he would return. I don't know where you are on this spectrum.

Hopefully you are somewhere in the middle, closer to the dance of victory.

If you are allowing your thoughts to constantly go to memories of your ex and wondering what happened, then please stop. You are allowing your ex to live rent-free in your head, and you are just creating a mental prison for yourself. He is probably moving on having a great time, and you are miserable and suffering.

I don't say that to be mean. I say it because I want you to realize that you are worth so much more, and you deserve so much better. It breaks my heart to think that you have spent even one day being sad. I want you to live a happy life. The Universe wants you to live a happy life. Obsessing over your ex is not going to bring you happiness, and it won't bring him back either. If you are stuck in this space, please use the tools at the end of this chapter to help you.

If your ex did move on and is with someone else or has remarried, please try to remember this. He is trying to heal too. For some people, forgetting is the only way they know how to heal. They have to move on quickly because they can't stand to be alone thinking about the failure of your marriage.

Everyone moves through pain in different ways. You are taking the time to properly heal yourself. I think that is courageous, intelligent, and freaking amazing.

You are doing the right thing. Taking the time to heal yourself is the bravest, smartest, and most productive thing you can do. Not only will you heal yourself, but you will also ensure that your future relationships are exactly what you want.

You deserve a relationship where you are cherished, respected, and made to feel secure. Don't settle for anything less than that. Just remember that the right person for you is on the way.

Be Civil

If you do have interactions with a new stepparent or girlfriend of an ex, try to be civil in as much as that is possible. This is not a negative thing because your children will just have more people to love and care for them.

They can actually be a very big help to you if you allow it. It's another person who can be available to pick them up from school or an activity when you can't. This person most likely wants to have a friendly relationship with you as well.

If you are in a situation where the other partner is unkind, know that it says something about that person's character. That person is probably just jealous that you had a relationship with your ex and that you had kids together. It's still important to try to get along.

You don't want your children to be put in a situation where they have to choose sides. It's important for you to try to get past the ego and let your children know that it's OK to love you both. This may take time and effort on your part to get to this point.

I completely sympathize with you, but it is super important. You will have a new partner eventually too. You want your kids to love your new partner when they meet, don't you? Think about it from that perspective.

Just make sure you do not compare yourself to the new girlfriend/spouse because that is totally unproductive, and if it makes you feel better, that says something about your character. If it makes you feel worse, that also says something about your character. It says that you have low self-esteem. When you are happy with yourself and your life, you don't give a rat's you know what about what anyone else does or is. I can't tell you how freeing that feeling is.

If you made it this far, then you either didn't care about your ex (just kidding) or you are already going to work on freeing yourself from him. Either way, good job. I know this topic isn't an easy or pleasant one. It can be super tough, especially in my case when my ex forgot to mention that he had a fiancée and got married. That was fun.

My kids had to be the ones to tell me, and I felt terrible that they were the ones put in that position because I could see on their faces that they didn't want to hurt me. I had to try to hide my shock and pain, and I'm not so sure I did such a great job of that.

I never want my kids to have to do something like that again. It was totally unfair to them. Keep that in mind when you start dating again. Your partner shouldn't hear about things like that from your kids first. Have a responsible and mature conversation with your ex before your kids meet someone new. I'm not saying you have to run and tell your ex about every guy you date, but if it gets serious enough to meet your kids, you should at least let their other parent know.

You should both try to be adults about this, especially for the kids' sake. After all, a stepparent isn't replacing the love of a biological parent. It's just one more person to add to your child's inner circle. Kids need all of the love they can get. In the end, having more people in your child's life should be a blessing, not a curse. Try to see it that way if you can.

JOURNALING MOMENT

WHAT WAS THE LESSON?

It's time for a journal assignment. Write in your journal, "What lesson was I supposed to learn?" Put that
question out to the Universe, and then sit in stillness
until the answer comes to you. Don't worry if it
doesn't come right away. Your answer may even
come to you while you sleep, so pay attention to your
dreams and also signs around you.

You may hear repeated phrases or songs. Pay attention to the things you are seeing and hearing repeat-
edly. You could also ask to be shown through God's
eyes what this is all about. Ask, "God, what behaviors am I repeating that need to end?"

I promise you that there is a lesson here. The good
news is that once you have learned this lesson, you
don't have to repeat it again.

AFTER-JOURNALING REFLECTION

HEALING TOOLS

If you are feeling emotionally stuck or tied to this past relationship, then I suggest you do a cord-cutting. There are many great guided meditations for cord-cuttings on YouTube. I also have one on my podcast, "Awaken Your Inner Awesomeness."

You could also do an EFT tapping to clear yourself of emotional pain. If you are feeling stuck or tied to the relationship, it could be because you need to learn a lesson. You may be repeating a pattern of behavior that you need to break.

You can also do a past life regression to see if you are repeating behaviors from past lives. There are some free guided meditations for this on YouTube as well. Take the time necessary to work through this situation. You will be glad that you did.

I would also suggest that you ask Archangels Michael, Uriel, and Raphael to help clear you of any past emotional trauma. I'm including a sample prayer.

A Prayer to Archangels Michael, Uriel, and Raphael:

> *Dear Archangels Michael, Uriel, and Raphael,*
>
> *I am feeling so lost right now. I feel sad, hurt, and sometimes alone.*
> *Please help me to see the lesson in my divorce, and please help me to let go of the hurt and pain that it has caused.*
> *Allow me to free myself of the emotional burden that I am carrying around with me.*
> *Help me to forgive my ex and myself for any pain we have caused each other.*
> *May we be able to raise our children in cooperation and love.*
> *Help me to let go of any fears that I have about my future and this situation.*
> *Help me to feel whole once more.*
> *Thank you for allowing me the opportunity to learn and grow from this.*
>
> *Amen*

8

DO I REALLY HAVE TO

DEAL WITH THIS JERK?

*I*f you find yourself going through a divorce, chances are that you have probably experienced the joys of fighting with your ex over issues regarding your children, division of property, you name it.

Everyone's experiences with their exes are different, but I'm sure that we have all experienced some commonalities no doubt.

For mothers, if you didn't have those beautiful children, then you could simply walk away from your ex without a second thought and never have to see his stupid face again, but you do have them—and you love them immensely—so you have to figure out a way to deal with your ex that is healthy for both you and your children.

So, how do you do that without having a stroke or accidentally stabbing someone? I'm asking for a friend.

Dealing with an ex can be a very frustrating thing. I understand that better than you know, but the most important thing that I can stress to you right now is not to put your children in the middle of anything... I mean anything.

Those kiddos are innocent and should be able to feel as though they can love you and your ex equally. This is not always an easy thing to do (especially if your ex is an asshat), but it is so important.

I fell short with this sometimes. If I was frustrated with my ex, I might express that in front of the kids (I always tried not to, but I am human), which put them in an awkward position. Of course, my ex also said bad things about me to my kids as well. We both failed here.

In as much as it is possible, never say anything negative about your ex in front of the kids. In fact, even if it is difficult, try to say positive things about him. Bring up nice memories from time to time.

It will help your children see that they have both of you and it's OK to love you both equally. No child should feel as though they have to choose between parents. This extends to your ex's family as well.

Don't say negative things about their grandparents or other members of the family, and make sure that your family and friends also follow this rule.

These are all people that your children love and should love. When you say negative things, it puts them in the position of having to defend those they love. That will only make them resent you. Don't ever put a child in that position. Seriously, don't even put a grown-up in that position. It sucks, and it is not cool.

~

BOUNDARIES WITH YOUR EX

Earlier, I talked about having healthy boundaries with people. Having a healthy boundary with your ex and his family is so important. This is another issue that causes problems for many divorced parents raising children together.

When my kids were little, I tried to continue to spend time with my ex and the kids together. I thought that I was showing the kids that we both loved them enough that we could be around each other so they would have us both. I was totally wrong.

What it did was confuse my kids, made them feel like they needed me around all of the time, and it gave my ex-husband hope that we were going to get back together again. This wasn't good for any of us.

I'm not saying that later on you couldn't do things with your ex and your kids, but it can be very confusing for young children and you when your divorce is so new. It can be a confusing time for you because you may feel romantic feelings for your ex.

When you are around them and enjoying yourself, it is like it was when you first met. You tend to forget about all of the things that made you want to get divorced in the first place, or if you are the one who wishes to get back with your ex, then you may be setting yourself up for further heartache.

It would be very easy to fall back into old habits and patterns, which I mentioned in a previous chapter is not good for you. You left those old ways for a reason. They weren't serving you. Remember, the rear-view mirror is small for a reason.

You really have to establish healthy boundaries before you ever start thinking about doing things together again. When your kids are older, they will understand things better. You will also be less likely to want to get back together with your ex if you are no longer in a vulnerable place in your life.

You can feel especially vulnerable right after a separation. Loneliness can set in, and your hatred of all things having to do with dating could make you want to retreat to the comfort of your old situation. The more time you have apart, the less vulnerable you will be.

If you do decide to get back together with an ex, it doesn't mean that it's wrong. That's why establishing a healthy boundary in the beginning is so important. If you do decide to try to make it work, then you will know it was a decision made for the right reasons and not out of sadness, loneliness, emptiness, or fear.

Unfortunately, too many of our decisions are fear-based as it is. I think many people end up back together with an ex because they feel like they can't make it on their own. I feel very sad about this because so many people don't realize just how strong they are. You should never need another person to make you feel whole.

I'd like to point out one last thing that I feel is very important. If you are spending a lot of time with your ex, then you won't be available if a better partner comes along. Your energy is closed off from receiving new love.

Furthermore, if you are dating again, your new partner might not appreciate you spending a lot of time with your ex, which is totally understandable. You can't make room for someone else in your life if you already have a person filling that space. Like I said, it's a confusing time for everyone.

Be Flexible

Holidays can be another issue that causes strife for newly divorced couples. How do your children get to spend time equally with both sides of the family?

Hopefully you had a really good divorce lawyer, who carefully outlined that in your custody agreement, but I would like to add that it is nice if you can be flexible with each other during the holidays.

The children will certainly appreciate equal time with both families. Try to focus on what's good about the holidays and let go of the disappointments. There will be things that pop up during the holidays that can make sharing custody more difficult. Like your relatives flying all the way from Australia to see your kids, and they can only see them on this particular day at this particular time, so again be flexible.

Try to see the positive in being together with your kids and your family. Try to be accommodating when you can, and make it pleasant for everyone. You want to make sure that you leave your children with good memories, not therapy bills. You will make mistakes ... it happens. Just remember that every day is a new day to start afresh.

Always try to do your very best. Always try to do all things with good intentions. If you are having issues with your ex, try to meditate, do some tapping, or ask your angels and guides for help. Whatever you do, do not get sucked into an emotional pit, or you will find yourself on the couch with ice cream eating your sorrows. No one wants that.

I mentioned earlier that if you work on shifting yourself, those around you shift as well. This can also work with your ex. You can become better at communicating with each other in areas that involve the kids. This is definitely a win for you.

Share Responsibilities

Earlier, I talked about how important it was to take care of yourself. Make sure that you aren't solely responsible for everything that involves the kids. Share the responsibility.

Just because you are now divorced, it doesn't mean that your ex is any less responsible for your children. Let him step up and help you with things regarding the kids. Make sure that you are both equally taking care of them.

I know that in some situations this is not possible. Don't leave your children with an ex who is taking drugs or is an alcoholic. If you do find yourself in this position, I sympathize with you. I had full custody of my kids, and I did more than my fair share, which nearly burned me out. It wasn't because my ex wasn't capable of taking care of our kids. I just ended up doing most of it. I should have been better about asking for help.

If you can't rely on your ex, please try to find people who can help you. It's not a weakness to ask for help. Remember the example of the past life lesson. It simply means that you realize that your own mental and physical health is important too. You can't be there for your kids if you are so stressed that you have nothing left to give them.

On the other hand, if your ex is capable of taking care of the kids, then let him. This will allow you to take some time for yourself. It will also teach your children that they can come to you both if they need you. How awesome is it to have more people to love them?

Setting rules for two different homes is another sticky widget in the wheel of divorce. If you are no longer with your husband, it could be because you have differing opinions about raising your children, or maybe you have different values. That definitely happens. This can make the job of raising children together very complicated.

Children need rules and structure; in fact, they actually want that. If you have one set of rules for your house and another set of rules for Dad's house, your child will likely be very confused and frustrated. That is logical. It would be hard to remember which house has which rules. It will be very frustrating for you both as well.

If you don't allow your children to use your couch as a trampoline (for obvious reasons), yet your ex does, then you are going to get really irritated when your child comes home and uses your couch as a trampoline. It's not your child's fault though.

If it is at all possible for you to be civil and reasonable with your ex, and sometimes it is not, you should try to get together and come up with a list of basic rules that are important to you both. (You have to be discerning here. Jumping on a couch could be dangerous, but leaving a cup on the table is not. Pick your battles.)

Make a chart for your kids. Let them know that these rules will be enforced in both homes, and make sure you come up with reasonable and just punishments as well. This doesn't mean that you can't have a few additional rules at your house. It just lets the kids know that these are the rules that have to be abided by in both homes because the rules will ensure that they are safe.

Make sure you back each other up too when it comes to punishment. Playing good cop/bad cop is not good for anyone. The kids will learn which parent they can manipulate, and they will also resent the parent who is the constant enforcer.

The good cop parent isn't doing their child any favors by being lenient. He/she is being a doormat, and that is going to backfire for that parent when the children get older. They will not respect that parent. The other parent will resent having to be the bad cop. I can tell you from experience that it is not a fun role to be the bad cop.

OPEN COMMUNICATION

At some point, when the divorce is no longer fresh, you could sit down and talk to your ex about your divorce and what happened. This isn't something that you have to do, but it may bring you peace or closure and may make you feel better.

I believe that we are all here on this earth to learn. What better way to learn than to find out what the other person was going through and how you got to where you are? It doesn't mean that you should feel guilt or blame. Leave those emotions out of it. That is the kind of baggage that I was talking about that we bring from past lives. You need to let go of those emotions, which you can do through EFT or meditation.

Keep the conversation strictly business if you can. Imagine that you were just a casual observer of your marriage. This is helpful because you leave the emotions out of it, you can actually deal with the true issues. If you aren't capable of talking to your ex without becoming upset or feeling overly emotional, then there is no need to do it. The point is to help you feel better, not worse. It is perfectly feasible to learn and grow through other methods.

One final suggestion that I would make to help you keep your household running smoothly is to sit down with your kids and talk to them. Ideally, you and your ex could sit down with them together and explain what is going on.

Divorce can be a very confusing time for children, but they are smart enough to realize that something is different about their home. They will listen, and hopefully you can help them understand that your love for them has never changed and will never change, even if your household is changing.

Unfortunately, my children were too young to have this conversation. They never knew a different way of living other than their parents being divorced. It still would have been a good idea for us to talk to them. I think it would have benefitted them greatly.

If you have tried all of these things and you still feel as though your children are having a rough time adjusting, then you may wish to consider taking them to counseling. Counseling is a great way for kids to express their emotions in a safe and non-threatening environment.

Most kids do not like the idea of having to go to counseling, but if you explain to them that it is going to help them feel better and that it is perfectly normal, then they shouldn't resist as much. If you have to, you can drag them kicking and screaming. I'm just kidding. Please don't do that. I'm sorry to all of the counselors out there.

The main thing to remember here is that you and your kids are going to be OK. If you follow the steps mentioned above, you should ensure that your kids will feel loved and secure. That is the most important thing that we can provide for our children.

I know that you are a good parent and that you want what is best for your child. Your child just wants to be understood and loved. That is really what it boils down to. There are a lot of people who love and care for you and your children, such as your angels and guides just to name a few.

You can ask your angels and guides to help your children as well as you when you pray to them. I'm sure that you probably already pray for your kids every day anyway, so why not ask for additional healing for them? Your angels and guides are happy to do it. They love you so much.

9

MANIPULATION, MONOPOLY,

AND OTHER FUN GAMES

*I*f you have ever been caught in the crossfires of manipulation, then you know that it is indeed not a fun game. It is stressful, hurtful, and downright frustrating.

I felt led to include a chapter on manipulation in my book because I know how much of a toll it took on my own life and how hard it was to break free from. Manipulation is nothing more than a glorified power struggle.

When someone is trying to manipulate you, either through emotional tactics or, worse, your children, they are trying to steal your personal power. It can be hard to detect when someone is manipulating you. It can be even harder to stop the manipulation dead in its tracks.

Stop Participating

I am going to let you in on a little secret though. Like a game that is being played, manipulation only works if you have two willing participants. You may be wondering what in the world I am talking about. Let me explain exactly what I mean.

I already talked about how my ex-husband would cry or use emotional warfare to manipulate me. He also employed other tactics as well. He would call my cell phone at all hours of the night. There was no emergency, and he didn't need anything, he just wanted to be able to do something that would disrupt my life.

My family all suggested that I turn off my phone. This would have been a simple solution, and the problem would have been solved. The problem was that I used my phone as an alarm; I didn't have a house phone, so I needed this phone in case of emergency—and why should I have to turn off my phone anyway, Karen?

He was not going to win this fight. I participated in this little game for a while; in fact, I participated for far too long. My counselor told me that I had a choice in this matter and that if I stopped reacting, it would no longer be fun for my ex.

That made sense, yet I thought it had to be too simple. Just exactly how did I stop participating in this little game of manipulation? I relied on common sense, oh, and the law. I went to my local police station to file a complaint. As it turns out, there is a law stating that you can't harass someone by phone. Who knew? Karen probably knew. She is a know-it-all after all. How annoying.

Now that I knew the law was on my side, I formally filed a complaint, and they issued a cease and desist letter. I never heard anything more about it from my ex, but the calling stopped. I was finally able to get a good night's sleep. Well, as much sleep as a mom of twins can get.

~

STOP REACTING

I also found other ways to stop participating in his awful game. I learned that by not having an emotional reaction to things that were said and done to me, I could end the harassment. You may be wondering how you can even do that.

I know that not reacting is difficult sometimes; in fact, it can seem nearly impossible to do. It is absolutely necessary, though, if you want the manipulation to end. The reason that your ex or anyone else does mean things to you is to control you. You are allowing their actions to control your reactions. You react to their stimulus, and they steal your personal peace and power.

Think about the classical conditioning experiment with Pavlov's dogs. In this experiment, Pavlov wanted to see if he could cause the dog's salivary glands to produce saliva at the sound of a bell. He had to produce food first along with the sound of the bell because the dogs wouldn't react to the bell alone.

The dogs had to have a stimulus in order for their salivary glands to react. The stimulus was the food, and the food was the initial catalyst for the salivary glands to react. Manipulation is somewhat the same. You have to be provided a stimulus for your emotions to react. If Pavlov's dogs stopped salivating when the bell was rung, then he would have stopped the experiment and considered it a failure. He wouldn't have gotten the reaction he wanted.

In the same way, if you stop reacting to the stimulus that is presented to you (the stimulus is whatever your trigger is) your ex will give up and consider this experiment a failure too. No one is going to expend energy doing things that yield no results. Therefore, it stops being a fun game when there is no one to play with.

If you stop playing this game, your partner will stop too. Remember when you were a child and your friend got mad, took the ball, and went home? The game had to stop because there was no ball. This is exactly the same concept.

When we stop reacting emotionally to what goes on around us, it stops being fun for our manipulators. The only way for someone to manipulate you is to know what your buttons are so they can push them and get a reaction. Someone can't push your buttons if they don't know what your buttons are. Thus, this fun game becomes a frustratingly failed experiment. You keep your peace, and your manipulator loses. That's a win in my book.

This can be a very difficult road to navigate, so have patience with yourself. If you do forget and react, don't lose hope, all is not lost; you can still do better next time. It's a process of retraining your brain, so it may take some time for this to catch on. You can do it though.

If your ex decides to use your children as tools in his game, this may make things more challenging. It's really sad that someone would use children to play a game of manipulation, but it does happen. It happened with my kids. I understand that it is frustrating, but I promise you that even this will end if you stop reacting to it.

This doesn't mean that you can't react behind closed doors. It simply means that you can't react in front of the person trying to manipulate you. You may have to pick your battles and decide that it is worth losing once in a while (without reacting) in order to end the manipulation. You may have to give up certain things with your kids temporarily.

As I said before, it isn't easy. If you are like me, you have probably reacted emotionally to situations that were out of your control your whole life. What I have learned is that reacting emotionally and getting upset isn't helpful in any way. It's not good for your health, it isn't solving any problems, and it just gives the other people or situations that you are reacting to your personal power. Don't give up your personal power to anyone or anything.

If you ask yourself this question, "Will this matter in a month, a year, five years etc.?" you will probably see that it won't. Therefore, if something isn't going to affect your life in the long term, then don't allow it to steal your energy or power in the short term.

You can do this, and once you have learned to stop giving away your personal power, people will not continue to try to take it because they will know that it is a waste of their time.

10

KEEPING YOUR SANITY

There are many things that can contribute to a sense of being in balance or take away from our sense of balance. The good news is that we can control most of those things.

Having a healthy balance in life will not only ensure that you keep your sanity, but it will also protect you from getting sick. When we run ourselves ragged, we tend to lower the function of our immune system, which is what is protecting us from getting sick in the first place. You are also less likely to feel depressed and anxious if your life is in balance.

If you are a parent, there are so many facets in your life that you need to think about when it comes to balance. We have to make sure that we are paying equal attention to work, our kids, our social lives, our spiritual lives, and our romantic lives.

We expend different amounts of energy in each of these areas on any given day; however, the overall amount of time we spend in each of these categories should balance out. If any one of these things is taking up more time than another, you are likely to feel off-balance. If you neglect one or more areas, you are going to be at risk for creating havoc in your life.

Take a tripod, for instance; if one of the legs is shorter than the others, the tripod will most likely fall over. In the same way, if any of the aforementioned areas in your life are neglected, then it will affect other parts of your life, and it will create a domino effect. It could impact your health, your social relationships may suffer, or you could suffer from increased anxiety or stress.

Unless you were born independently wealthy (if you were, can I please be your friend?), then you likely have to work in order to provide for your children. The reality is that in today's economy most families require two working parents in order to survive.

This means that during the hours you are working, you have less time for your kids. For most people, the child's school day also coincides with the parent's work day. In that case, parents are still able to be there for their children before and after school, which is great.

Work can be a very stressful thing. It's important to ensure that your career isn't taking up the majority of your time. It's also very crucial that you are able to leave work at work as much as possible. If you are bringing your work home, then it is hard to give your kids the undivided attention that they deserve. They really just want your time with them to be uninterrupted.

If you are working yourself to death, this may be a time for you to really examine whether or not you need a career change. I know the thought of change is scary, but it may be necessary. We were not put here to work our fingers to the bones. So, it's important to ensure that work isn't taking up all of your time. That is a sure-fire way to stress yourself out and become sick.

~

Choose Balance

Being parents, we are often tasked with the responsibility of taking our kids to all of their extracurricular activities. This just comes with the territory. It's part of our job as parents, and we love watching them excel for the most part. It becomes a problem, though, when we are too busy running from one activity to the next.

I see so many parents who want to sign up their kids for every sport or activity there is. I understand the logic behind this. This doesn't just apply to single parents either. You want the best for your kids, and you want them to experience everything they can. You feel that you are expanding your child's horizons. Those sports also help them get scholarships for college. They get to meet new friends, and if they are busy, then they can't get into trouble, right?

Yeah, that may be true to a certain degree, and your intentions are good, but I think that you may be overlooking a very obvious point. When your child is that busy, and you are that busy, you are both going to end up burned out. You are going to be exhausted. You are going to be a total mess. Even the thought of setting foot outside your bed will make you want to cry your eyes out. You will meet yourself coming and going, which is going to throw your life severely off-balance.

It's incredible to think that much of the chaos in our lives is self-created. We want to be there for our children and show them how much we love them, so we sign them up for every activity that they want to try. It's great to be supportive of your kids but not to the point that neither of you can function.

When your children are young, it can be overwhelming for them to have to be at two to three different practices several times a week. Plus, it gets really expensive. Furthermore, your child probably has homework for school that he or she has to keep up with on top of going to practices. We all know how mean those teachers are. They assign tons of homework.

Has your child ever whined that they didn't want to go to a practice? You probably just chalked it up to being tired or having a bad day. What if your child is really trying to tell you something? Maybe they really are tired ... too tired to keep that schedule.

The best practice is to let your child pick one or two sports or activities that they really want to focus on. This doesn't mean that their interests won't change and that they have to stick with the first thing they picked. They can choose to do something different when the activity they picked is over.

Exposing them to a variety of activities is also good. It gives them a choice and allows them to see what they enjoy. In real life, your child wouldn't be able to do 20 different activities as an adult. They would burn out. Sticking to one or two activities teaches them how to be picky with their time.

You don't want your child to grow up to be an adult who is stressed out because they try to do too much. Teach them balance as a child. It's one of the best gifts we can give them because it's something they will need as an adult.

You're reading this now because you are probably having a difficult time yourself trying to find balance. Helping to teach your children balance will benefit everyone in the long run. You will also have happier children, and you won't be stressing yourself out as much either.

Take Time for Yourself

Learn how to take time out for yourself. You need to go out with your friends and have fun now and then too. If you share custody of your children with your ex, then you can do this when he has them. Ignoring your social life is also very harmful for you.

We need time with our friends to relax, de-stress, and just laugh our asses off. It helps us to let go of some of the stress in our lives, plus our friends are great at listening and giving good advice. Having a healthy social life is important.

You don't want to neglect your friends, and they will be good to remind you that they never liked your ex anyway or that you are too good for him. You can also roll your eyes about the stupid things that Karen has done or said lately. You're feeling better already.

Remember earlier when I talked about how you need to let your ex help with your kids? You can also use the time you have when he has them to work on the things that you need to do to take care of yourself.

One of those things is learning how to relax. Take time to do the things you love again. I like to read, go for walks, or sometimes just watch TV. It's hard to do some of those things when you are constantly taking kids to practice, helping with homework, cooking dinner, etc. It's nice to have the time to yourself again. You deserve to have a little time off now and then. You need time to rest and get rejuvenated.

You can be a much better parent to your child if you aren't tired and emotionally drained. Your children want to see you happy.

Taking time out to take care of yourself and to get rest will benefit the whole family. Please don't neglect yourself. You take care of everyone else, and it's time to take care of you. You deserve to feel whole and happy, which you will not feel if you do not take time out for yourself. It's not selfish. It is essential.

It is so important that you don't neglect your spirituality as well. Again, one of the reasons why we go through difficult situations is to experience spiritual growth.

We may all have different spiritual beliefs; however, I believe that it is important that we all have some type of belief system. We usually get our spiritual beliefs from our parents, but we do not have to keep those beliefs if they don't resonate with us.

If you have a church that you attend, that is awesome. I hope that you will continue to attend and pray each day. It really can be uplifting and give you positive messages to take with you for the week.

If you don't have a church or you aren't particularly religious, I would recommend daily meditation and prayer to feed your spiritual growth. I meditate and pray daily, and I can't tell you how great that makes me feel.

Maybe now is a good time to re-examine your beliefs and whether or not you wish to explore new beliefs. There are so many great resources out there. Hay House has a great library of awesome educational tools. There are also some excellent podcasts about spirituality out there that are free.

I just feel that our spiritual team, which includes God, our spirit guides, and our angels, wants us to be more mindful of our spiritual growth. They love us and want to help us achieve our dreams and goals, and they want us to be exuberantly happy.

Spending some time on your spirituality will help

keep your life in balance. Moreover, you can say a prayer to Archangel Haniel to help you find balance and assist you in creating your new beginning. Haniel is associated with the colors pearl blue and white. You may sense or see these colors as you work with Haniel. Working with our spiritual team can help relieve our anxiety and give us a sense of tranquility.

The final area of your life that you should not neglect if you want to have balance is romance. You really deserve to find love again. So, when the time feels right for you (and you will know), get out there and start dating again. Aside from loving yourself, you also have a need as a human being to experience love from others.

Remember those butterflies that you get in your stomach when you are around someone you are attracted to. That is a freaking awesome feeling. I know you want to feel that again.

I also know that it can be scary to put yourself back out there once more, but you will never experience the good feelings if you don't take the risk. The important thing is not to avoid this area of your life.

I waited for a long time to start dating again because I had too many good excuses not to date. I had some doozies like my kids need me, I don't have time, and other BS like that. In reality, I was too scared to put myself out there again. I had a huge fear of rejection. So, I let that area of my life go. That was not the best decision that I have ever made.

My kids deserved to have a mom who was happy. I would have been much happier if I hadn't neglected this area of my life, so please take my advice and spend some time on your love life. If you are scared, there are tools out there that I will discuss in other chapters that you can use to help you alleviate those fears.

The final point that I would like to make is this... Time goes by way too fast as it is. If you are constantly running around like a chicken with its head cut off, you are going to miss the best parts of your child's childhood. You most certainly do not want that. Their precious faces only stay little for so long. Before you know it, their voices deepen, they grow 50 feet in height, and they are eating your whole refrigerator.

I think that God wants you to know that He blessed you with your children, and He wants you to enjoy the time you have with them. Don't be concerned about trying to do all of those extra activities all of the time. Take time out to cherish the moments with them while you can. Spend quality time together, laugh, and play because you will never regret doing that.

11

YOUR NEW NORMAL

*W*hat is normal? That word gets thrown around a lot, but what does it really mean? Who or what is normal these days?

You are going to have to figure out what normal looks like for you now, and that is OK. It is a process that we all have to go through after divorce. Your normal may not look like anyone else's normal and that's OK. My point is that we are all different.

One thing that I have found to be true in life is that you should never compare yourself to anyone else or live someone else's idea of the perfect life. That is not constructive at all, and you have no idea what someone else's life is really like anyway.

Many people are extremely good at hiding what is really going on in their lives and putting on a brave, albeit fake, smile. You're not fooling anyone, Karen. If you really wished your life was like Karen's, you might be wishing for some terrible things without even knowing it. I heard her husband drinks, but you didn't hear that from me. Besides, someone may have thought the same about you once without realizing that you had your own stuff to deal with.

Don't try to be your idea of what someone else's normal is. I can't stress enough the importance of using this opportunity to figure out who you truly are. Live your own great life. Be original. How many sequels are really better than the original anyway? I mean *Empire Strikes Back* was better than *Star Wars*, but that is so rare. I wonder how many emails I'm going to get telling me how wrong I am. Oh well, nerds.

As I mentioned, your new normal should include time doing things just for you. As women, and as single moms, we can sometimes get so caught up in doing things for others that we forget to do things for ourselves.

You are so important. You need to take care of you. That includes your spiritual you as well as your physical you. Take time to do the things you enjoy. What is it that you enjoy doing?

What Is Your Passion?

If I said to you, "You can take the whole day off to enjoy doing anything you want," what would you choose to do? What is your passion? If you can't answer either of those questions, then maybe you need to start by figuring out what it is that you do enjoy doing.

Try new things. Join a book club; take a language class; paint; go for a hike. You get the idea. Get out there and see what speaks to you. You may find a new hidden passion that you never even realized existed. What if you uncover a hidden artistic ability? You could have been Van Gogh all along, minus the missing ear, and never known it.

Pamper Yourself

It's important to keep the vehicles that drive our souls around in good running condition. I'm talking about our bodies, of course. You need to take care of your physical body. I mean Olivia Newton John even sang a song about it. "Let's get physical..." That song was totally about working out, right? I mean everyone in the music video had workout clothes on. Hmm, I wonder why my aunt wouldn't let me listen to that song.

Anyway, you would never drive your car for 15,000 miles without getting an oil change. You don't do that, do you? Your poor car. Just as your car needs scheduled maintenance, so does your body. Schedule time to pamper yourself. I like to go get massages now and then. It is definitely an easy way to feel relaxed and rejuvenated. If a massage isn't your thing, then go get a facial. Go get both if you feel like it—go wild. Get your hair and nails done. Join a gym. Pamper yourself.

FEEL FREE

If money is tight for you, and I hope it is not, there are many free things that you can do for yourself that will do wonders.

An easy way to relax and unwind is to take a hot bath with Epsom salts and maybe a few drops of an essential oil. Many places sell inexpensive bottles of essential oils these days. Add any fragrance that you find soothing. Put on some relaxing music and just soak. Soak away all of those worries.

Go for a walk or a bike ride and get out in nature. Sometimes just reconnecting yourself to Mother Earth can help you feel grounded and centered again.

Move!

Exercising is a great way to take care of yourself, and it will make you feel better. I mean maybe not when you are doing it because you'll be sweating and maybe in pain and maybe cussing at the instructor ... but afterwards you will feel great.

Exercising releases endorphins, and you may lose weight in the process too. You're going to be so hot, and your ex is going to be so mad that he let you go.

You don't have to pay for an expensive gym membership in order to work out. You can find some awesome workouts to do at home. All you need is a yoga mat (you can get inexpensive ones almost anywhere) and weights. You can even fill water bottles up with sand if you don't want to spend money on weights or use cans of vegetables, which you probably already have in your cabinet.

There are so many excellent and free workouts on YouTube as well. Find one that you like. Mix it up. Do a different routine each time. Do some yoga. Yoga is great for stretching, increasing flexibility, clearing the mind, and centering yourself. Now there is even this thing called hot yoga. I don't know what it is, but it sounds pretty hot.

~

SPIRITUAL SELF-CARE

Just as your physical body needs rejuvenation, so does your spiritual body. You can continue to do the things I talked about in Chapter 3 like EFT, meditation, and listening to music. Journaling is another great way to release your emotions.

I also think that it is important to find a group of people who are like-minded spiritually. They can help you to grow and develop your spiritual self, and isn't that what we want? If you already belong to a church, then great. Continue to be involved and seek community with those members.

If you are not affiliated with any church or religion, just know that you have a whole spiritual team of angels and guides who want to help you on your journey. All you have to do is ask them. You can ask them for guidance and assistance. They will readily hear you and assist you. You just have to be willing and open to hear their guidance and to feel their love.

There are many Facebook groups and online communities out there, too, that are full of people who want to support you. All you have to do is go and find them.

I know that some of you may be reading this and thinking, *I don't want anything to do with religion or spirituality.* I understand that too. If that it is you, here are some great tips that you can use that do not involve religion or spirituality.

I mentioned that there are many supportive Facebook groups out there for single parents. There are also a lot of great reading materials and articles online about single parenting and self-care. Just do a Google search for articles on single parenting. I already mentioned a few of the books that I read that helped me with my parenting skills.

There are so many great self-help books out there. There are also many counselors who specialize in divorce and single parenting situations. The important thing is to find someone you trust and can confide in.

∾

Mindfulness

Even if you are not religious, it is important to work on breathing and mindfulness. Meditation is such a great way to de-stress and relax. It lowers your blood pressure, and it can help you sleep better at night. Mindfulness is something to which many successful people attribute their success.

Having a positive attitude and outlook on life can change the way you see your situation. If you can imagine your life as beautiful, then you begin to see the beauty in everyday moments. You begin to see that anything is possible.

∽

TIME WITH YOUR KIDS

When you are having a particularly emotionally draining day, and you just need a time out, find something fun for your kids to do that will entertain them and give you a break. I used to take my kids to the local library for story time. It was great because they were entertained, and I could sit for a few minutes and rest.

There are also some great programs at the local YMCAs. They are pretty inexpensive, and they teach great social and emotional skills. I put my kids in the gymnastics and rock-climbing classes. The great thing about this was that while they were in class, I could work out in the gym myself. It was awesome because I was getting exercise and so were they. I would watch them for a bit and then go get my workout in.

Our city also has a program for parents and kids. They offer classes where parents and kids can interact together. They have classes like ballet, karate, and tennis. In addition, one of our local grocery stores offers parent/child cooking classes. These are great programs that allow you to spend time with your kids, and you get to enjoy the activities as well.

~

Time with Your Friends

As I mentioned before, it's important to spend time with good friends too. They make us laugh and can provide a great listening ear when we need it (and they don't charge $100 an hour).

I think it is good to have friends of all ages. Older people can give us some great advice and make us laugh at how stupid they think our society has become. What is up with those millennials anyway? Additionally, younger people can help you understand the way that society around us is shifting. They can probably help you set up your dating profile in no time flat too, and they can help you perfect your selfie game or explain to you why Snapchat is such a big deal.

People our own age can make us laugh talking about how much hairspray we used in high school, or we can wonder together why banana clips went out of style. Really, why did those go out of style? They were so easy to use.

Just having people who love and support you is so important. Laughing is probably one of the best ways to forget about how pissed you are at your ex too. Laughter really can be the best medicine. There have been studies that show that it does wonders for you medically. It releases endorphins, lowers stress hormones, and increases immune cell production.

Furthermore, it's just plain awesome to laugh. Laughing so hard that your side hurts is one of the best things in the world. They even have laughter yoga. I did not make that up. I seriously didn't. Stop laughing.

Maybe grab some of your best girlfriends (or guy friends) and go to a comedy club. You can laugh and have fun. Plus, if you go hang out with your friends in cool places, it is possible that you could meet some awesome people ... maybe even a cool new date.

12

HOW TO KEEP YOUR KIDS

OUT OF JAIL

$\mathcal{Y}$ou probably read the title of this chapter and thought, *Are her kids in jail?*

No, they are not, but it is one of those looming fears that all parents have.

We beg, "Please don't let us screw up our kids so that they grow up to become serial killers." We pray and worry for our children and hope that they will be safe. Every parent worries that they are not doing a good job with their kids.

Honestly, it's the parents who don't worry that I would be afraid of. If you think you are the perfect parent, you are kidding yourself. I don't know any perfect parents. Karen thinks she is perfect, but she is so delusional, and her kids are nightmares.

Don't let your worries about your parenting overcome you. Don't forget that we talked about how you manifest your thoughts. So, stop worrying about the unknown. We can't control that anyway, and you don't want to call those things into being. Focus on the here and now.

Your job is to love your kids unconditionally, to provide and care for your kids, and to establish your parenting norms now so that your house runs smoothly. That's all you can do. The other stuff is probably just your own anxiety and fears getting in your head. Your ego is likely running the show. Stop going there. You are going to do a great job with your kids. I know that. It's obvious that you care about them or you wouldn't have all of this anxiety. Look at Karen's kids. They're a mess.

ESTABLISHING RULES

You may be wondering how to establish norms when it comes to your children. I mentioned earlier that you need to have rules because children want them. It's true that they want structure. Structure makes a child feel safe, and they know what they can expect. It will also help you keep your sanity. Have you ever seen *Nanny 9 11*? I'm having anxiety thinking about all of those wild kids running around with no rules.

Depending on the age of your children when you divorce, you may have already had rules established in your home. If you did, that's great. Keep enforcing them. You may need to adjust them a little too. That's fine. If you didn't, well, here is your chance to start.

One way to establish rules is to think of all of the things that you need in order for your house to run smoothly. This can be making sure that your kids pick up after themselves (so you can keep your sanity and not lose it every time they leave a dirty dish out) or ensuring that they don't jump off of the roof because they could break a leg.

Only you know what rules you need to have in order for your house to be peaceful for you. The important thing is to make sure that the kids are safe and feel loved. Come up with a list of your rules. It might be lengthy at first, but we are going to work on making those more manageable.

How do you whittle down those rules to a manageable number? I mean it really isn't reasonable to have a list of a hundred rules. Your kids' heads will explode. You need to compile a list of manageable rules.

It's also a good idea to involve your kids in the rule-making process. You could take the list of rules that you have (which is probably too long anyway) and ask the kids to help you decide which rules you need to keep and which to discard. They will help you to prioritize your rules.

In so doing, you are allowing them to see the thought process behind the rules. They will hopefully realize that *Mom is making this rule to keep me safe and not because she's mean and doesn't want anyone to have fun ever.* It also allows them to have a stake in the rules. They will feel more empowered by this.

You could have some "do" rules and some "don't" rules. Here are some examples: Do sit when eating dinner. Don't hit your siblings. You may also have some situational rules like rules for when riding in the car.

In addition, come up with a list of fair consequences with them. Ask them what they think a proper punishment should be if they don't put away their dirty dishes. You may not get the response you hoped for. They may say something like, "I think that I should be grounded for 10 minutes." You will probably want to roll your eyes. You may even become frustrated. Hang in there; you can guide them to an appropriate punishment.

You could say something like, "Now Billy, do you honestly think that 10 minutes without video games will help you remember not to break the rules again?" Hopefully, they will take this seriously and come up with better punishments. This again will allow them to have a stake in the process. I think they will resent the rules less if you take the time to do this.

Again, it would be great if you could involve your ex with this too, but I also realize that this is not always possible.

~

PRE-ESTABLISHED PUNISHMENTS

Creating a list of rules is great, but it is useless if you do not enforce them. That is something that I was not always good at doing. I was the bad cop all of the time anyway, so sometimes I felt like if the infraction was so small I wouldn't enforce the rule. I didn't want to be a nag. I should have been better about enforcing the rules. Stand your ground here. Your kids will thank you for it later.

If you ensure that the punishments you have set aside are reasonable and fair, then it won't be as difficult to stick to the punishment. Having a list of rules and punishments is invaluable because you don't have to think of on-the-spot punishments.

This is where so many parents get into trouble. They get angry because a child broke the rules, and so they yell, "You are grounded for a month." This really isn't reasonable, and now you either have to stick to the punishment or back down and look weak. Either situation is not ideal.

Having pre-established punishments will relieve some of your headaches in this area. An important thing to remember is that punishments should not block children entirely from their social circles.

In other words, don't take everything away from them all at once. You can still let them go to sporting events or activities. Totally isolating your child is not a good thing. I learned this the hard way. My son resented me a lot when I took away all of his forms of communicating with friends.

Some psychologists also suggest giving kids options for earning back their freedoms earlier. This is totally up to you. You have to be OK with whatever you decide. I have done this before with my kids, and it worked well for me. They had to do a certain number of good things in order to cancel out the punishment a little early. Think of it as time off for good behavior.

Once again, this has to be something that you are comfortable with, and the things your child has to do to earn back the time have to be something that would merit early release from punishment, not something they would do anyway. Making them apologize to someone is great, but I'm not sure that this alone warrants early release from punishment. That's another thing that it would be helpful to establish ahead of time, the kinds of things your child can do to earn back their freedom.

If you are totally flabbergasted at how to come up with rules (and you may be), remember we weren't sent home with a parenting manual. There are a lot of really good parenting books out there with great suggestions.

You may not have come from a traditional home where rules were established. We all grew up differently, and I think our generation had a sort of hodge-podge of parenting styles. That is not to say that any one style is good or bad, but I know that, for me, it was difficult establishing rules because I felt like my own household didn't necessarily have established rules.

Don't get me wrong because I knew what would cross a line and result in getting punished. However, I was from the generation of "Do it because I said so." I understood that if I kept crying and throwing a fit, I was going to get something to cry about. Does that sound familiar? It probably does. This is what our parents knew, but it really didn't help me understand why I was expected to follow certain rules.

We didn't have established rules, and I certainly never assisted in creating those rules. It was sort of trial and error. That can be confusing and frustrating for a child. Having this background made enforcing rules for my own kids very difficult. My kids were too smart to fall for the "because I said so" crap.

You may be experiencing the same thing. Do a little research about general rules for kids. Keep what resonates and works for you and get rid of what doesn't. You don't have to have the same list of rules as someone else. You have to consider what behavior you are and are not willing to put up with.

Talk to your friends and see what they do or go to one of those online support groups and ask others what they do. Again, I stress that you should keep what resonates with you and leave what doesn't.

~

KEEPING ROUTINES

If at all possible, it is also important to establish routines with your children. They should know that at this time we eat dinner, bedtime is at nine, or that homework gets done right after school and then you can go play. This goes along with having rules, but it's amazing how quickly we can get away from routines, and that is not good for kids either.

They need that stability, which is especially important in cases of divorce. Their life hasn't been so stable lately, so they need to feel like they can count on a few things for certain.

I mentioned earlier that rules should be established in both households. Routines should also be established and be similar if possible in both households.

We live in the real world, though, and I am not naive. I understand that this won't always happen. My kids would have totally different routines at their dad's house, and I know this had to be hard on them. They were allowed to stay up later, eat more sugary food, and other things they weren't allowed to do at home.

I remember that it was hard on me as a child going from one house to another. Rules and routines were totally different for us in each home. We normally ate dinner at four or five at my mom's house, but then my dad got home from work later and we had to drive an hour to get to his house. Our dinner there was usually much later. That used to be very frustrating to me as a child. I was hungry, and I wanted to eat at a certain time.

Obviously, because of real-world constraints like a job, my dad couldn't help that we ate later. My point is this—make every effort to establish routines that they can count on.

13

WHAT THE HECK DOES A HEALTHY RELATIONSHIP LOOK LIKE ANYWAY?

*U*nhealthy, codependent, or imbalanced relationships are becoming more and more common these days. I know I was a pro at unhealthy relationships. If it were an Olympic sport, I would have taken the gold many times. I'm the Michael Phelps of bad relationships.

Seriously, though, the simple reality is that healthy relationships are extremely important. I believe it is one of the main reasons we are here on Earth. We are learning how to navigate through these waters.

Unfortunately, if you had a childhood that was anything like mine, then you didn't even know what a healthy relationship actually looked like. I didn't have a normal healthy relationship modeled for me at home, and I know that my mom probably didn't have one modeled for her either.

We learn from what we see in our environment, so if you didn't grow up seeing a healthy relationship, then you probably don't even know what one is. I thought I would devote this chapter to helping you discover what a normal, healthy relationship should be like.

Here is a little disclaimer though; I am only going to be scratching the surface. There is so much information out there. I simply wanted to be able to give you a few pointers. I am imparting years of research and money spent on my part to you for the very low cost of this book. You're welcome. Not you, Karen. You can spend your own money and do your own research.

~

Know Your Types

The first thing you need to understand is what type of person you are being in a relationship. There are two main types of people.

There is the person who is more passive, giving, artistic, introverted, and sensitive. This person is usually an all-around people pleaser. This person will tend to give more of their share in the relationship, which can lead to frustration and resentment because this person feels like they have been taken advantage of.

The other type of person is more self-focused, stubborn, extroverted, confrontational, or direct. This person is usually the one who is in charge. This person also has to have his or her own way.

There are other qualities here for both types of people, but I think you get the idea. You can be a mixture of both, but you will tend to have more qualities of one than the other. The reason it is important to know this is because if you are the person who tends to be a people pleaser in the relationship, you can become lost in the mix of a partnership.

In fact, it becomes less like a partnership and more like a dictatorship because one person is calling all of the shots, while the other person is doing the heavy lifting in the relationship. It can become very easy to lose your own identity. This will cause you to become extremely frustrated as well.

In a balanced relationship, you should be two separate people. You can certainly share some of the same friends and interests, but you should also have friends and interests outside of the relationship. There is also equal give and take in a healthy relationship. One person isn't doing all of the work.

Let me give you a visual example here. Think about an eclipse. The moon totally covers the sun, and everything goes crazy. Your relationship should not look like an eclipse. You should not be so together that you cover each other up and block out everything else.

You should have your own separate identities. It's perfectly healthy to do things outside of the relationship with other people. It is extremely vital that you don't disappear in the relationship. You need to remain your own individual person.

ATTACHMENT STYLES

Another important issue to think about in a relationship is the type of attachment you tend to form with people. There are four main attachment styles: secure, avoidant, anxious, and anxious-avoidant.

Knowing what type of attachment style you have can tell a lot about how you behave in a relationship; for instance, it can explain how you deal with closeness and intimacy. It also reveals how well you are able to communicate your needs in relationships, and it can determine your ability to deal with conflict as well.

Our attachment styles are formed when we are children. It stems from the connection we form with our parents and caregivers when we are young.

The following traits are of people with a secure attachment style:

- Low on avoidance.
- Low on anxiety.
- Comfortable with intimacy.
- Not worried about rejection.
- People with a secure attachment style generally do not fear getting close to someone or fear being abandoned.
- Most likely had warm, caring parents who were sensitive to their child's needs.

People with an avoidant attachment style usually display the following traits:

- High on avoidance, low on anxiety.
- Uncomfortable with closeness. Really wants to have independence and freedom.
- Not worried about a partner's availability.
- Most likely had emotionally unavailable parents who were disengaged or detached.

People with anxious attachment usually display the following traits:

- Low on avoidance, high on anxiety.
- Desires closeness and intimacy.
- Is very insecure about the relationship.
- Is hypersensitive.
- Most likely had inconsistent parenting.

*I used to see myself in this particular attachment style. It can definitely cause problems when you are with someone who has the secure or avoidance style.

People with anxious-avoidant attachment usually display the following traits:

- High on avoidance.
- High on anxiety.
- Uncomfortable with intimacy and worried about their partner's commitment level in the relationship.
- Likely had past emotional trauma or abuse as a child.

Can you identify your own attachment style from above? It says a lot about how you behave in relationships. Our old childhood behavior and thought patterns are totally affecting the way we show up in our current relationships.

That is why it is so important to understand how and why you behave the way you do. The attachment style that you formed when you were very young is controlling the way you act in your relationships now.

As you can see, if you have two people with very different attachment styles, the relationship can become very complicated rather quickly. It may even seem like you are trying to speak two very different languages.

Knowing your attachment style can help you understand why you communicate or behave the way that you do in relationships. It can also point you in the right direction for correcting that behavior.

I had an anxious attachment style, and I had to learn how to stop feeling so insecure in my relationships and to give my partner space. I learned that the behaviors I thought were going to help keep my partner in the relationship were actually driving him away.

Changing your mindset and behaviors is possible. It takes work, but it can be done. Once you know what type of attachment style you have, you can find resources online for how to understand and change those behavior patterns.

LOVING YOURSELF

Another thing that you need to understand is that your actions in relationships could actually be blocking you from receiving the love that you deserve. You may be unintentionally attracting people who are emotionally or even physically unavailable because you are afraid of getting hurt.

This goes back to those old limiting beliefs about love and the type of attachment you formed with your parents. Here we go blaming moms again. I'm just kidding. The main piece of advice that I can give you here if you are insecure about love is to work on your own self-love. If you come across as desperate or lonely, then you will actually repel potential partners or even attract the wrong ones.

When you love yourself and are secure in who you are, no one can mistreat you because you simply won't allow it. You also won't try to chase anyone because you will know your worth. You see, goddesses don't have to chase people. They are the ones who are chased.

Another key factor in successful relationships is developing the right connection with an ideal partner. When you are in the beginning stages of a new relationship, it's important to make sure that you are striving to form a true connection.

Ensure that you feel good about yourself because that is what will attract your perfect partner, and when I say perfect partner, I mean perfect for you. When you exude happiness, confidence, gratitude, joy, and peace, you will become even more attractive to potential partners, like that goddess I mentioned above.

~

SPEAK UP

It's also important to make sure that you are showing up fully and engaging with your partner in the relationship. Be yourself and share your opinions. No one likes a person who just agrees with everything you say. It's boring. They're dating you because they want to know more about you and what makes you tick. So, show them that side of you.

Learn how to pick your battles too. Sometimes, when you are both tired and it's been a long day, arguments can spring up over silly things. Decide what is truly important to you and what you can be flexible about. If something does happen to be important for you, say so.

It's your responsibility to speak up when things don't feel right in a relationship. If you don't say anything, you will just be filled with resentment and hostility, which will then blow up into a big argument.

Don't avoid conflict just to make peace, also know

what is worth speaking up about and what is not. Leaving the toilet seat up may be a trait you are just going to have to live with; however, making you feel like a lesser person is not something you should ever live with. Know when to speak up and when to be flexible.

The most important thing to remember about a relationship is that it should be fun. You may meet someone when you least expect it because when you are out there living your life and having fun, people see the energy that you are exuding. They want to be around that. You will attract others just by enjoying your life.

As I mentioned earlier, there is so much more to know about relationships, but this is not that book. If you are interested in learning more, please find experts who can help you in this field. There are a lot of great books out there about relationships. The book *The Five Love Languages* is a great place to start.

Healthy relationships can be a lot of hard work, but they are worth it. They're worth the time and effort that you may have to spend to learn more about them. You are worth the time and effort spent to have a healthy and happy relationship.

14

JUMPING BACK IN

*D*ating after a divorce can be a very daunting task. I liken it to jumping out of an airplane without a parachute, except even that isn't as frightening.

The thought of having to get back out there and date made me feel anxiety like I had never experienced before. My friends and family insisted that I had to get back out there again. I could tell that they thought I was going to end up being a crazy cat lady, except I had no cats, which is even more pathetic.

"You have to get back on that horse," they would say. Well, what the hell does that mean anyway? I don't want a horse. I want a man. On second thought, a horse is probably easier to deal with than a man ... never mind, I don't think a horse could fit inside the door of my favorite bar. I could have a lifetime designated driver though... I guess that still isn't a good idea. I needed to find an actual real human man. Ooh, that sounded desperate. I was definitely not desperate.

I would like to state once again that I do not believe that you have to have a romantic partner in order to lead a happy life; however, romantic partnerships can be very fulfilling. It's not that I didn't want one. I had just put up so much armor around my heart that I truly didn't think it was possible for me to find someone again.

I was wrong, of course. I had to let go of my fear and jump into the deep end of the dating pool head first and somehow manage not to hit my head and drown. So, then came the next issue, which was how to meet someone.

The way I met my ex-husband was through a fix-up. My family knew this guy who was so great. Thanks a lot, guys. They still apologize to me to this day for that. Just kidding. He did have some good qualities, and we made some pretty awesome kids, so it wasn't a total wash.

You may have friends who think they are doing you a solid by setting you up with every single guy they know. What I found out about my friends is that we have very different tastes in men.

Yes, a third nipple does bother me. No, I don't enjoy listening to hours of Yanni. No, I'd prefer not to sample your bathtub beer. You get the idea.

If you do decide to go out on a blind date set up by a friend, it can be pretty awkward when you let the date know you have zero interest in dating them ever again. Like, if I never saw your face ever again, that'd be great.

I'm not saying don't go out with friends of friends. It is possible to meet someone this way. Just be careful about that. Whatever you do, do not let Karen fix you up with someone. She would probably set you up with a psychopath. This is Karen we are talking about.

So, how do you meet people? In today's technological world, the answer seems to be online. This is probably a very different experience from how you met guys before, at least it was for me.

You may be thinking to yourself, *Hold on there, sister. I am not ready to start dating again. I am terrified at the very thought. I would rather get a tooth filled or have a mammogram.* I get you. I was you.

You have to jump back in at some point, but I understand that you may be feeling some anxiety. Just don't head to the couch and curl up in the fetal position. It's going to be OK. You will meet someone in due time, and it's going to be amazing.

Ease Anxiety

Your fears are not irrational because we tend to put armor around our hearts once we have been hurt, so it's natural that you may be feeling scared or anxious. You can overcome this though.

The first thing you need to do is to get rid of that armor and ease that anxiety, which is really just your ego spewing those limiting beliefs at you. Ego simply stands for Edging God Out.

God wants us to experience so much love in our lives. When your ego steps in, you need to remember that it is just telling you lies to keep you from receiving all of the things you deserve. You deserve to find love again, so tell your ego to shove it and let's go already.

You can do some tapping exercises to heal your broken heart. I think this is such a funny expression because our hearts go on beating perfectly fine after a breakup. We just need to remember that. Our hearts don't really break. It's still there doing its job of pumping our blood.

You can also do some meditation work to quiet your fears about dating again. If you put yourself out there, it is possible that you may get hurt again. I wish I could promise you that you won't, but I can't. What I can promise you is that if you don't try again, you will never experience the pure joy that is the love of another human being. It is so worth it.

Decide What You Want

Before you jump back onto the dating scene, it's important to know what you hope to get out of a relationship. Most people never even take the time to figure out what it is they truly want in a partner. So, how do you know if you've found it?

I suggest that you make a list of all of the things that you want and don't want in a relationship. Make two columns in your journal and just start listing what comes to you. Don't worry about it being too long. Is your list two pages long? Boy, are you picky!

I'm kidding of course. You really should be a little picky. I mean if you just put down that you want a man, you could end up with someone like Charles Manson. He is a man after all. You didn't specify that you didn't want a psychopath, so how can you expect the Universe to know that you didn't want a psychopath? Geez, picky much?

Seriously, though, we do have to let the Universe know what we want. God loves us and wants us to have exactly what we want, but we have to work with Him a little here.

When you have finished making your list, go back and look at it again. This time I want you to think of all of the things you need in a partner. What will make you feel happy and secure?

These are the things you absolutely need to have in a partner. Look at your list again and cross off the things that aren't needs. These are qualities that would be nice to have in a partner but aren't deal breakers if your partner doesn't have them.

For example, I would like to have a rich partner, but it isn't a deal breaker if he isn't a billionaire. I'll settle for a millionaire. Seriously, though, be realistic. Your list should hopefully be smaller now. If it isn't, maybe you're being too picky, princess?

Do the same thing for the things you don't want column. Go through and see what qualities you absolutely cannot live with. Cross out everything else. These are qualities that you don't necessarily want in a partner but they aren't deal breakers.

Another example here is that I would not date

someone who smokes. That is a deal breaker, so I would keep that on my list. I wouldn't necessarily pick a guy who plays video games, but if he happens to enjoy it, it's not a deal breaker.

Now look at the list you have again. It should be more manageable by now. If it isn't, then good luck finding Prince Charming, Cinderella. I'm kidding, but you really should make sure that you aren't being unrealistic about what you expect. You are looking for a *human male*, not a superhero. We all would love to date Chris Pratt, but I'm pretty positive that he doesn't know or care who I am.

Keep this list in mind as you are looking for a new partner. It's important to know what you need in a partner. You wouldn't go shopping for shoes without considering your taste and style, so why would you go shopping for a life partner without being as discriminatory?

DO SOME GROUNDWORK

Another thing that I would suggest that you do before you get out on the dating scene again is some emotional and spiritual groundwork. You may have some things that you are doing that could be keeping you from having healthy relationships. I know I did.

One of the things that I discovered about myself was that I have a fear of rejection, which I'm sure stemmed from my dad leaving when I was young. I tried to be too accommodating in my relationships (in order to avoid being rejected), which resulted in me giving more than I got.

It also caused me to resent the guy that I was dating because I had unrealistic expectations of him. I expected him to match my energy and give as much as I did. Another result of this was that I came off as needy, which made me less attractive. Neediness will make a guy run and scream in the opposite direction faster than you can say, "Commitment."

I caused the exact outcome that I was hoping to ward off. I could have totally avoided this situation if I had just been myself, had confidence, and spoken up for myself. That is a pattern that I kept repeating in relationships. I didn't speak up for myself, and I wasn't authentic enough. You may have experienced this as well. You have to know who you are and be prepared to speak your truth. Be your authentic true self.

You should never have to change who you are to please someone else. You may be afraid that your partner might find out that you are not perfect, but remember we all know that there are no perfect people ... even Karen.

CHOOSE WISELY

You may also tend to pick guys who are emotionally or physically unavailable to you or who lean on you financially. This is also a road to disaster. Your partnership should really be 50/50. He should want to be there for you, and you should want to be there for him.

I remember in one relationship I went to get a massage. My boyfriend at the time texted and said something like, "It's a good thing you have a boyfriend who spoils you." I paid for and set up the massage myself. I'm not sure what part of that situation said that my boyfriend spoiled me, but this is exactly what I'm saying you need to avoid. You need to avoid men who think they spoil you by doing nothing out of the ordinary for you. I guess in his mind I was spoiled because I allowed myself to get a massage?

It was a weird statement, and I should have done what my gut said and told him exactly why **he** was the lucky one to have me. I know my worth now, and I definitely do deserve a guy who spoils me, not someone who just says he does. Remember ladies, actions speak much louder than words.

Take an Active Role

You have to take an active role in your love life and decide that you aren't simply going to allow life to happen to you. Don't just hope and pray for someone or blame others because you don't have someone yet. You have to do the work.

Get rid of those pesky limiting beliefs about love. Take a long look at what your behavior looked like in past relationships. Why do you behave that way? Is there an underlying fear or limiting belief that is running the show? Chances are there is.

Depending on what limiting belief you hold, you need to do some work to get rid of it and change your mindset. Take accountability for the problems in your relationships that were caused by your behavior.

It's important to remember that you are only doing this reflection to see what you could do differently or better. Do not start that game of being self-critical. Do not beat yourself up over mistakes that you have made. Just look at your behavior and see if you notice some patterns.

If you can, look at it from the perspective of an outside objective observer. You are simply trying to discover whether or not you have any patterns that you seem to repeat in your relationships that you need to break.

I know that you really want to find someone again, and you totally deserve to. If you do the work don't let the word "work" scare you; it need not be tedious, and it will make you feel better. You will find someone who deserves you and cherishes you.

In addition to being too insecure and not speaking your truth, another thing that could be happening in your relationships is that you might be acting too pushy by trying to control everything that happens. You are probably also trying to avoid a breakup, but you are really causing it instead.

When you are being pushy or controlling, you are giving off a masculine energy. Do you really think a man is looking for masculine qualities in a woman? No, he is not. That energy will turn him off for sure.

Think about your behavior in your previous relationships. How did you behave in them? Were you too needy, too accommodating, or too pushy? You want a healthy relationship where both you and your partner are financially and emotionally stable.

You may see other couples out holding hands and

looking so in love, and it may really make you feel bad because you don't have that. Don't get stuck on wanting what others have because you, too, are going to find someone who will love you so much. Those kinds of thoughts will lower your energy vibration as well.

Instead, change your thoughts to: *I can't wait to meet the man who will hold my hand like that or look at me like that.* You will meet him someday, and you will be so thankful that it didn't work out with your ex.

Remember that you are the key ingredient in attracting your soul mate. You hold the power within you. Make sure that you are taking care of yourself physically, emotionally, mentally, and spiritually.

If you are emotionally or physically drained, you aren't going to have the energy to really give to a partner or relationship. Be your most authentic self and be prepared to communicate your needs.

Remember that the energy you put out is the energy you will receive. If you give off a desperate energy or feel bad about yourself, you are going to attract a man with those same qualities. You get what you give is really a true statement. Make sure that you are healthy, whole, and complete before you go out and start dating again. Put your best energy forward.

~

ASK FOR HELP

We can also ask our spiritual team for help in bringing our soul mates to us. You can ask for this when you pray or meditate. Don't get bogged down by the specifics when praying for your soul mate. Do you really want to limit the Universe to bringing you someone with blond hair and blue eyes? There could be an awesome dark-haired, brown-eyed guy out there for you, but you keep asking for a blond. Be open to what your soul mate could look like or be like.

The Universe knows what we need. I would simply thank the Universe for sending you your soul mate, who is perfect for you. Keep it short and sweet. Be sure to show your gratitude for their work on your behalf.

Don't get stuck on a timeline either. I know we want everything to happen yesterday, but it may take a while for you to meet your soul mate, and there are several reasons why this may occur. Your soul mate may be working through some things himself, so maybe he isn't quite ready to meet you. He may have to work on his low self-esteem.

Also, you may need some practice dating before you meet him because it's been a while since you dated, and you may need to work on your flirting first. You may need a few practice make-out sessions to remember what it's like to feel passionately about someone.

It's also possible that you still need to work on issues within you, and dating may bring those issues up for you, which is good because you can resolve them before you meet your dream man.

Remember to be patient. I know that you are anxious to find someone, but let me give you an example of something that happened to me. I met a guy online when I first started dating again. He was a great guy, and it turned out to be a very serious six-month relationship.

Through this relationship, I found a few things that triggered some fears and emotional insecurities inside of me. We ended the relationship, but this relationship was a gift because it is what led me on my spiritual journey and helped me to realize what I needed to heal within me before I could completely and unconditionally love someone else. I would never have known that I still needed to work on myself if I hadn't had that relationship.

There are some other things you can do to help you attract and keep a loving relationship. You can wear rose quartz crystals or place rose quartz crystals in your home to help you attract love.

You can also ask Archangel Chamuel to help you

find a loving relationship. He appears as a pale green color, so you may see this as you pray.

Here is a sample prayer to Chamuel:

> Archangel Chamuel,
> *I know that I am worthy and deserving of a
> loving and healthy relationship, so I ask for
> your assistance in bringing my soul mate
> near me and to me. I love myself completely
> and unconditionally, and I give out this same
> unconditional love. I am open to receiving
> and giving love unconditionally, not just in
> my romantic relationship but in all of my
> relationships. Please bring me my twin flame
> so full of love. Please guide me and show me
> the way to love and happiness. Please bring
> me my lover, my rock, my best friend. Thank
> you, Archangel Chamuel, for leading me and
> guiding my steps.*

Say this prayer every day, and then watch what happens. You can also ask Archangel Raguel to help you maintain harmonious and peaceful interactions and communication with your partner. Raguel appears as a pale blue color.

The most important thing is not to stress about this. Your spiritual team wants to send you someone who will make you happy, and when it does happen for you, you are going to have a permanent smile on your beautiful face.

GETTING PHYSICAL

Another important issue to think about before you start dating again is sex. Did that get your attention? I thought it might.

Having a healthy sex life is key for any healthy adult. Chances are you haven't had sex in a while if you are recently divorced, especially if your marriage was rocky. You may not have wanted to sleep with your ex for the last part of your marriage, and that is normal. Are you blushing? Stop it.

I don't know why people find it so difficult to discuss sex. Our society for some reason makes us feel guilty about that. Stop that right now. You do not need to feel guilty about sex, whether talking about it or doing it.

It's a normal human function, and it's important to know how you feel about it. You have to be OK with the decisions that you make for yourself. In order to know how you feel about it, you have to talk about it.

How do you feel about having sex? When should you have it? These are normal questions to ask yourself before you get back out there again. The days of feeling like you have to wait for marriage are over now for you anyway, aren't they?

Here is what I want to tell you, and, honestly, I feel as though I have been guided by spirit to tell you this. It is totally up to you to decide when you want to have sex with someone. It doesn't matter if it is your first date or your 23rd date. The choice is totally yours to make. You have to feel good about the choices you are making for yourself.

In this day and age, many men want to have sex faster, so if that is not you, speak up. You control your own fate here. You tell a guy if you are ready or not. Do not let a guy pressure you into doing something you aren't ready to do. Don't worry about whether or not he will not call you again because if you aren't ready and he doesn't respect that, forget him. What a loser he is.

You have to go into it knowing what might happen if you choose to have sex or not. Just make sure that you are being safe and that you are protected. Make healthy choices.

Having sex again after you've only been with the same partner for a while is going to be messy. It will probably be awkward and bumpy at first, but it's just like riding a bike. You never forget how. Hopefully, you just upgraded that bike (wink wink).

The right person will understand, and he will make you feel supported. Do not let anyone else make you feel bad for what you want to do with your body. That is your decision. It is no one else's business, so if you need to get your groove back, go get it, girl.

You are the master of your own destiny. Don't let anyone else hold the key for you. You will know when it is right for you. Don't feel guilty about it. Sex should be something to be enjoyed, so enjoy it when it is right for you.

Now that we got the awkward conversation out of the way ... make sure that you have taken the steps to get yourself ready for action. (I was talking about dating. I don't know where your mind was.)

Online Dating

Now that you have asked your spiritual team to help you, have done the emotional work, and you know what you are looking for in a partner, it's time to start dating.

As I mentioned earlier, the easiest way to meet people in today's society is to date online. If you have been out of the dating game for a while, this is a whole new ball game. Online dating is a completely different dating world from the one I was used to.

A friend sent me this meme, and it is so funny and maybe a little true. It says, "Afraid of not getting what you ordered with online shopping? Try online dating." Just a little humor. It's not really that bad once you get used to it.

However, at first, dating online brought about a whole new set of anxieties for me. First, you have to decide which dating site to use. Are you going to use Lots of Fish, Croissants and Cappuccino, City Slickers Only, or Atheist Mingle? Are you only going to try one site, or do you do what men do and use all of them simultaneously?

Which picture do you use as your profile pic? You want to attract the right kind of guy and not a serial killer. You want to look like you are fun but not too fun, if you know what I mean. I'm a mom after all.

Do you use a photo with a filter? If you use a filter to take away the bags under your eyes from lack of sleep but then show up for a date with the bags under your eyes from lack of sleep, you'll be accused of false advertisement.

If you use a photo taken with a Snapchat filter, then he will think you are 12 or an idiot. Why is it so hard to take a decent selfie? I can't get the angle right. How do people do it?

Now you find your perfect photo ... the one that you

took with only a slight filter on it, looking up of course because you don't want that double chin to show.

Next, you have to write a biography. "You didn't say there was going to be a test on here! What do you write? How do you make yourself sound interesting in only 300 characters? The winky-face emoji that I just used to show how fun I am took up a character ... now I only have 299 left. I used a space; that took up another... Why do spaces count as characters??"

How do you find a way to show that you are intelligent, yet not stuffy; dignified, yet not pretentious; fun, yet not slutty ... you get the idea. Think of the anxiety of finding your perfect picture except with words. My English teacher never taught me how to write a perfect dating bio. I blame our educational system. I was not prepared for this!

Why am I stressing over this? Some men don't even bother to try to write a bio; could that work for me? No, because then he will think that I am unintelligent and have nothing to say. Plus, I usually won't swipe on guys who don't say anything because I think they're boring and have nothing to say. Back to the drawing board.

You finally nail down that perfect bio, the one that says, "I'm the perfect catch." Wait ... does it say that? I'd better go check it again for the 100th time. Wait, I used that emoji and those spaces... I don't have enough characters to say that. Well, it probably says something more like, "I won't kill you in your sleep, and married men swipe left." Yes, I actually had to write that. That's as good as it is ever going to get. He knows you won't kill him and you won't get a Neanderthal. Hey, some men don't even bother to write a bio!

So, you set up your profile. You made sure you set your age range somewhere between legal and not dead ... although if he's dead, maybe you would inherit some money. Forget I said that.

You set your distance filter to on planet Earth... Maybe we shouldn't rule out other galaxies. Really, there could be a galaxy where everyone looks like Chris Pratt. On the other hand, they could all look like E.T. Never mind, let's just stick to planet Earth. You're all set!

So, now you get to start looking at what's out there. Spoiler alert: You are going to have to swipe through a lot of frogs in order to get to the princes. We're talking bathroom selfies (toilets in full view), men in wife beaters, men at the gym flexing their arms, men with no teeth, men kissing their guns (I don't mean muscles, ladies. I mean men are literally kissing their guns. We're talking AR-15s), men who are married but whose wives just don't understand them, husbands and wives who are looking to broaden their horizons, if you know what I mean.

Yes, I am totally serious and am not making this up. You just got super scared, didn't you? Don't run away. No, don't go back to the couch with your ice cream. It's going to be fine. Besides, you'll have some great things to laugh about with your friends.

In fact, it could be fun to get together with your friends and look through these profiles together. I know my daughter got a lot of laughs out of doing this with me. In fact, she is the one who convinced me to do this in the first place, and it really helped us to bond. It's not exactly how I pictured we would bond, but whatever works. You just have to know how to weed through the garden of men to get rid of the ones you don't want. It can be a fun process. Are you laughing? Why are you laughing?

It's hard to judge a person from a profile, but that's your first impression of a person (that's why it gave me so much anxiety when I was making mine). What I found is that many men do not take that much time to set up their profiles, except that they painstakingly pick photos that are purposefully misleading. Well, some of them do anyway.

You just have to be realistic about this. You may have to go on some bad dates in order to get to the good ones, but you will never experience the good ones if you don't get out there.

I would like to stress something that I think is important. If you do not feel comfortable when you meet a guy, just leave the date. Don't worry about hurting feelings. You have to trust your gut. Most men are nice and aren't looking to harm you, but you can never be too careful.

Also, if the date just doesn't seem to be going well, then don't feel the need to drag it out. Just excuse yourself and leave. The most important thing to remember is to have fun. You are going out there to meet new people. You may make a new friend or two in the process. Not all connections have to lead to true love. You may find a kindred spirit as well.

The interesting thing about online dating is that you end up having to carry on conversations with multiple people. It can be overwhelming if you are not used to it. Everyone asks the same questions too.

"Are you married?" (Really with this question?) "Do you have kids?" "Where do you live?" "What do you like to do for fun?" Didn't you freaking read my bio? I spent four hours writing it, and you didn't even bother to read it? Men!

Sometimes you forget what questions you asked them already. Some men will match with you and then never strike up a conversation. I'm still not sure why they do this. I guess they just see how many women they can match. Some men want to jump straight from the dating site to texting on the phone.

~

Ease into It

Again, go at your own comfort level. If you aren't ready to move that fast, be honest. I always worried about hurting other people's feelings. I got over that really quickly, and it definitely served me well. I didn't want to waste my or anyone else's time if there were no sparks. You have to decide what is best for you. Always trust your instincts. They will never fail you.

The most important piece of advice I can give you is not to worry about it. Everything is going to fall into place when the time is right. Don't look at it with the attitude of, "I have to date now." Try changing that to, "I get to date now."

Have fun. Yes, it can be scary. Yes, you will probably have some bad dates. Yes, you could get hurt. However, look at the flip side. Yes, you will meet some awesome people. Yes, you will remember what it feels like to get those butterflies in your stomach again. Yes, you will get to laugh until your side hurts again. Yes, you will get to dream of someone else again.

Don't spend one ounce of your energy worrying about the bad stuff that could happen. Instead, focus all of your energy on all of the awesome things to look forward to. You are going to meet some amazing new people, and, one day, one of them will be your best friend.

I know it can happen for you because it happened for me, and I am so freaking amazingly happy. It's an awesome feeling to know that you found a partner in crime who loves you so incredibly much, showers you with so much affection, and is so super supportive of everything you do.

He really makes you want to be a better person inside and out, and you thank your entire spiritual team every day for bringing you such a blessing. You'd better get ready for that, girl. Not even Karen will be able to ruin your day when you find your soul mate. You guys are going to be so happy! Look at how cute you are together!

My Hope for You

I hope that this book helped you find your peace again. I hope that I have left you better than when we met, and I wish you every happiness in your life. You are a good person; in fact, you are an awesome person, and you deserve it.

The God I know loves you and wants you to be so happy and abundant in all areas of your life. All you have to do is set your clear intentions and ask for what you want.

Live in a state of constant gratitude for all that you have and all that you will receive. Be unapologetic about who you are. Love every inch of yourself. Be a shining light for others and spread love, laughter, and joy. I hope you dance!

One day, you will see that there was a purpose in your pain. You were broken open for a reason. You had to keep breaking your own heart in order to open it fully. When your heart opens completely, you allow space for the light to come in and fill all of your emptiness.

This light then creates the most beautiful glow. You may think that everyone is judging you for your cracks, but they will soon see the beauty of how you transmuted your pain and made yourself whole once again. They will see that you have become the most beautiful work of art.

Like a delicate piece of ancient pottery, your cracks are filled with glittering gold. You will finally recognize in yourself the treasure that you have truly become, and those around you can't help but see the beautiful transformation in you. Like a butterfly emerging from a cocoon, you will take flight with your stunning new wings and conquer the world.

REFERENCES / CITATIONS

Cherry, Kendra, and Steven Gans. "The Five Levels of Maslow's Hierarchy of Needs."*Verywell Mind*, Verywellmind, 3 Apr. 2018, www.verywellmind.com/what-is-maslows-hierarchy-of-needs-4136760.

"Four Styles of Adult Attachment." *Evergreen Psychotherapy Center*, 26 May 2017, www.evergreenpsychotherapycenter.com/styles-adult-attachment/.

McLeod, Saul. "Pavlov's Dogs." *Simply Psychology*, Simply Psychology, 8 Oct. 2018, www.simplypsychology.org/pavlov.html.

Sincero, Jen. *You Are a Badass*. Running Press, 2017.

Trei, Lisa. "Psychologists Offer Proof of Brain's Ability to Suppress Memories." *Stanford University*, Stanford University, 8 Jan. 2004, news.stanford.edu/news/2004/january14/memory-114.html.

GET FREE BOOKS!

LAUGH . LEARN . LOVE

We learn best when we laugh and act best when we love.

MotherButterfly Books are penned to tickle the funny-bone, nourish the mind, & open the heart. *That's what makes our books different, and why you'll love reading them.*

Join us online for free books, workshops, masterminds, moon circles and more.

www.motherbutterfly.com

ABOUT THE AUTHOR

Melissa Oatman is from Collinsville, Illinois.
Melissa is a spiritual life coach, Reiki practitioner,
teacher, entrepreneur, and creator of the podcast
Awaken Your Inner Awesomeness.

This mother of four, (two humans, two fur babies)
has spent her life devoted to teaching and healing
others. She uses her life experiences as well as her
educational training to help others heal from the
trauma of divorce and break-ups and to help them
live their best lives. Melissa has a Bachelor's degree
in German and Master's degree in Educational Tech-
nology from S.I.U.E. Melissa is also certified as a
Reiki practitioner and Past Life Regressionist.

www.melissaoatman.com

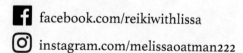

facebook.com/reikiwithlissa

instagram.com/melissaoatman222

Made in the USA
Columbia, SC
22 May 2024

36078045R00140